Reckonings of an FBI Agent

A Street Agent's Inspiring 31-Year Career

DAVID KAMEL

DEDICATION

This book is dedicated to my dad and his dream of becoming an FBI Special Agent. I didn't fully grasp my dad's dream, until more than a year after I retired when I found one of his love letters to my mom from while they were dating where he told her he was preparing himself for that day. My dad passed away in 2003, but saw his dream come true through his son in 1988.

A special thanks to the FBI agents and support personnel who have helped me achieve my successful and incredible 31-year career. And to my close friends who encouraged me to memorialize my stories in a book.

CONTENTS

AUTHOR'S NOTE

The stories in this book are true and reflect the author's recollection of events. Dialogue has been re-created from memory. Some individual names, company names, locations, and identifying characteristics have been changed to protect the privacy of those portrayed. These changes are depicted with an * after the name or location. Opinions are solely the author's and not opinions of the FBI.

DISCLAIMER

This book contains no FBI classified information. FBI cases mentioned in this book have been adjudicated through the judicial court process and are available to the general public through courts, news reports, public record searches or FOIA. Any reference to law enforcement tactics is considered common knowledge and is viewed as known acts published in the media or seen on television, motion pictures or videos. Any reference to FBI procedures is also considered common knowledge.

ACRONYMS USED IN THIS BOOK

AO – Area of Operation

ASAC – Assistant Special Agent in Charge

AUSA – Assistant United States Attorney

DOJ – Department of Justice

FBI – Federal Bureau of Investigation

LEO – Law Enforcement Officer

RA – Resident Agency (satellite office in an FBI division)

SA – Special Agent

SAC – Special Agent in Charge

SOG – Special Operations Group

SSA – Supervisory Special Agent

SWAT – Special Weapons and Tactics

THE BEGINNING

1

GROWING UP IN DALLAS

"A good agent does not go to trial" was a half-joking statement I often made to agents who were preparing for their upcoming trial. I counted on my investigative techniques, interview skills, and overwhelming evidence to obtain a guilty plea. I approached my subjects only when I had enough evidence to not only indict the subject, but to get a conviction. The subject would then be overwhelmed and quickly learned the preferable avenue was to plead guilty and avoid a lengthy prison sentence.

I grew up in far North Dallas. My mom was a stay-at-home mom. The house was always clean and in order. We rarely had dinner at a restaurant, but my mom was an excellent cook. We ate dinner together as a family every night. Never a frozen dish. If I woke up some morning not knowing what day it was and walked into the kitchen to find mom cooking pancakes, I knew it was Friday. Saturdays were either Mexican food prepared by Mom or steaks prepared by Dad. Every Sunday was Lebanese food my mom and sister prepared. All the home cooking was excellent.

We were a middle-class family and didn't have money for fancy vacations; all our trips except one involved visiting family. At any given time, my dad worked two or three jobs. He earned his college degree in finance at the age of 30 by attending night school. Dad was always working on home projects while I mowed the grass, stirred the paint or did whatever task my dad assigned me. I don't see this type of work ethic in the younger generations today. Sadly, I think we're beginning to see the results of this.

In 1974 I was 13 and it was about this time that one of my friends had a paper route, which sounded cool. I wanted a job, too, since my less than a dollar a week allowance wasn't adding up and I really wanted to have a car by the time I turned 16. When I look back on this, I'm glad it was up to me to earn the money to buy my own car. I learned a lot about the value of money.

So I got a paper route at 13. Since then I have always had a job, even through college, until I retired from the Federal Bureau of Investigation (FBI) in August of 2019. I began throwing newspapers for the Dallas Times Herald, which was established in 1888 and closed its doors in 1991. It was an afternoon paper, except on weekends, when it was delivered in the morning. I loved the freedom of the job. Weekends riding my bike in the quiet streets were exciting for a young teenager. After school, I would hop on my blue bicycle with two baskets on the back and one on the handlebars and ride to the newspaper drop-off location, which was at an apartment complex maybe a mile from our house.

I became an expert at wrapping newspapers with a rubber band and, if there was a chance of rain, stuffing them in plastic bags, which is the standard wrap today. As a rookie, I was given one of the least-liked routes, which featured an apartment building. It was indeed a challenge zigzagging my bike through the complex trying to throw newspapers to second floor balconies. Especially the Sunday newspaper. Most of the time I had to stop, get off my bike, lean it up against a wall, and throw the newspaper upstairs. I only broke one window, after an errant toss of a large Sunday morning paper. I waited after the crash to accept my punishment; it's not like I could get away with it. The man who lived there came flying out of his apartment and saw me and we both had a bit of a laugh. Turns out he was my math teacher, which was one of the few classes I excelled in besides history.

After several months, I was promoted to neighborhood routes, which was much easier. Plus, these neighborhoods were less than a half mile from my house. I didn't have a boss hanging over me all the time barking out orders. I had a route manager who trusted that I would not disappoint him or my customers. At the end of each month, I enclosed an envelope in the newspaper for customers to pay their bill. They could pay one month or several months forward by mailing a check to me. Very few customers paid several months in advance, but it was such a huge benefit for me when they did. If they didn't send a payment, I had to go door to door in the evening, collecting, which was a big pain. On more than a few occasions, I had to make several attempts to collect if a customer wasn't home or just didn't answer the door. Back then the price was $3.40 per month. Pretty darn inexpensive. When I was 15, about the time I quit throwing newspapers, the price had soared to over $4.00 per month. But during that time I had banked $3,000 in savings so when I turned 16 years old, I bought my first car for $1,500. It was a green 1970 ½ Camaro SS open front. I still drive through these neighborhoods and reminisce about those days.

What I didn't know then was that all my bike riding up and down hills, several miles a day, loaded with newspapers, would launch me into my great track and cross-country days, and later, prepare me for the rigors of the FBI. In high school I began working at a grocery store bagging and stocking groceries. Since my first car was still a year away, I'd bum a ride from my friend, Sonny*, who was a senior at my high school, JJ Pearce. JJ Pearce had some famous attendees, besides me. The most well-known would probably be Jessica Simpson.

Sonny was on the JJ Pearce track team… sort of. He was a broad jumper, and I would hang out with him by the track field waiting for him to finish practice and then catch a ride with him home. It was more like a social event than a sporting one. Cross-country season had ended and now it was track season. After a while, Sonny invited me to join the team and be a broad jumper. I had no spring in my step and I couldn't even come close to touching the bottom of a basketball net, but since I was there I decided "why not?" Each day we jumped in the broad jump pit until one day coach Daniel Winterten* who was standing next to the track yelled, "Kamel you are not a broad jumper. Come over here to the track. Let's see if you can run." Not knowing what I could do I started running and the next thing I knew I made the Junior Varsity (JV) team and then the Varsity team running the mile and two-mile.

At the time, JJ Pearce was in Texas' largest high school division which was 4A. My first year, which was my junior year, I was running the mile in 4:40 to 4:45. Not great, but good enough to compete in all the meets. I realized then that I was in good shape and fit from the years I pedaled my heavy bike every day, throwing newspapers rain or shine.

I guess you could say I found a calling, or at least a hobby. The following year, I made the cross-country team and in the first meet I became the number one runner on the JV team. It was difficult for me to make the varsity cross-country team, since our varsity team was one of the top teams in the state. In the late 70's the distance for cross-country in Texas was two miles and the meets were run on Saturday mornings at various parks or similar settings throughout the Dallas Fort Worth Metroplex. The following year, after I graduated, the cross-country race distance in Texas was increased to three miles.

Each cross-country meet, our team arrived early at the race site and if we didn't know the course, we walked it as a team. Each meet averaged over one hundred runners. The top 10 finishers received a trophy or a medal. I preferred the trophy. A team's top 5 runners were scored to determine a team's finish position. The lower the finishing position of the runner, the lower the score and better finishing position for a team. On the JV team, I remained the number one runner. The district meet was held in Dallas at Norbuck Park, which included what our team called "bullshit hill." We ran several meets at bullshit hill. At the district meet, I finished first and "broke the tape" for my first and only time. Our JV team finished first with a perfect score of 15. Including my first-place position, our runners finished 2nd, 3rd, 4th and 5th. Our varsity made state, which was held in Georgetown, Texas. The top two runners on the JV team also traveled to Georgetown as alternates. The alternates were only used if a member of the varsity team was unable to run in the meet for whatever reason. I was not needed.

The following year, my senior year, I was the number one runner on the varsity cross-country team. I held that position for each meet except for one in Arlington, where I finished behind a teammate. I wasn't happy with my performance. In cross-country, everyone on the team knew I had a strange running strategy in the two-mile meets. I didn't create or think up this strategy, but it worked for me. For the first half mile I ran in the back of the pack, but I would slowly start increasing my speed as the other runners were decreasing their speed. The other runners would usually start out in a sprint when the starter's pistol sounded. So as the race continued, not only would I began passing other runners, but I was also passing all of my teammates at different stages of the race. I began picking runners in front of me as a motivation to pass. It worked and I always finished in the top ten for a trophy or a medal. My two best race times for the two-mile run were 9:53 and 9:56. Mind you, running up and down small inclines and crowded spaces was more difficult than running eight laps on a flat track.

In 1979, my senior year, our team made the state meet in Georgetown with 13 other division 4A teams. Our team expected to finish in the top ten in the state, but we knew the teams from the higher elevations in West Texas had the advantage. My goal was to finish in the top 40 or, at worst, top 50. We traveled to Georgetown in an old green beater van. The morning of the race we arrived early, but for some strange reason we only walked about half the course. When the starter's pistol sounded, we were off and running. I started behind my teammates as usual and I felt my pace was okay, but after a while I wasn't passing any teammates and began to worry about how I was performing. I was passing other runners, but where were my teammates? Later than expected, I began passing my teammates one by one. As I was passing one teammate he commented "Where have you been?" Knowing that I usually pass these guys sooner, I began to worry that my pace was too slow. I picked up speed and passed the rest of my teammates, but since we hadn't walked the entire course prior to the race I was lost as to the remaining distance to the finish line. As I was running, I came up on one of our team's alternates standing next to the course, cheering me on. He yelled "You need to kick now!" I'm first to admit that I never had a speedy kick like great long-distance runners. So I kicked to about three quarters of full speed, thinking I was coming up on the finish line. After I felt the "bear jump on my back" I realized that the finish line was farther out, so I toned down my speed. Once I finally saw the finish line I gave it my all and passed a few more runners, but I knew I didn't finish well. My final position was 66th place. Okay, so I was 66th in the state of Texas in the two-mile run in the highest division in Texas. As large as the state of Texas is, I should have been content, but I wasn't. Our team only beat one or two other teams. We were all disappointed and pictures of me at the end of the race reveal a clear indication of how I felt. But the worst was yet to come as track season was next.

The end of the cross-country season was a little disappointing. We had two runners on our team who were Juniors, but their race of choice in track was the half mile. They were ranked number one and two in the state of Texas and ended up with scholarships to SMU and

Texas A&M, but they couldn't beat me in the two-mile cross-country meets. This really surprised me, but on the other hand I was a total failure in the half-mile race, so I ran the mile at track meets instead. Each track meet we arrived early at the stadium where the half-miler who never lost a race in Texas had his boombox cranked up while we stretched. He played and danced to Led Zeppelin like a crazy man. I don't know where he got all that energy. The other teams knew of him from the track teams circles in Texas.

While I was disappointed with my 66th place finish at state in cross-country, the track season was ten times worse. After the second meet, I was kicked off the team. First a little background on how this transpired. In my senior year I signed up for all my necessary high school class credits and I also signed up for college freshman English at Richland College. Rumor had it that freshman English at North Texas (now University of North Texas) was difficult. So I decided I would take care of this and be a step ahead when I entered North Texas. I signed up and began taking the course. Since I was in high school, working and now taking this college freshman English course, I set up a meeting with the high school student counselor to review all the classes I was taking. I asked him if it would be alright if I dropped one of my high school classes since I was taking the college class. I also told him I was on the track team. After looking over my classes he said it would not be an issue. So I dropped a high school course and went about my way.

At the first track meet I ran a 4:37 mile, which was not great, but in 1979 it was good enough and I was happy knowing that I could shave time off in the coming meets. After this meet, Coach Winterten called me into his office. He told me that he knew I was planning to attend North Texas and said that if I could bring my mile times down I had a chance to earn a partial scholarship. The next meet I ran a time of 4:27 and was very pleased. The following week Coach Winterten called me back into his office and I thought, "Wow, he's going to be pleased with my time and congratulate me for shaving ten seconds off my time." That was not the case. Coach Winterten came right to the point and told me that he received a notice from the University Interscholastic League (UIL) out of Austin. UIL basically is the ruling authority for athletics in Texas. UIL told Coach Winterten that I was ineligible to run on the track team, since I didn't have enough current high school credits. If I remained on the team, based on the UIL rules, this could jeopardize the rest of the team. I explained to Coach Winterten about the meeting I had with the school counselor and the fact that I was enrolled in college freshman English, but Winterten's hands were tied. He was very sorry. As the saying goes—some days you're the bug and some days you're the windshield. I truly was the bug that day.

Like me, my parents were upset and they tried to set up a meeting with the school counselor, but he wouldn't see them. Instead, they met with the school principal. Even though the student relies on the correct guidance of the school counselor, our counselor clearly under-performed that day. The principal told my parents that, according to UIL rules, they couldn't go back in time to correct the issue. That was the end of my high school track days. The dropping of the high school class was allowed, but the college course could not count as a credit to maintain a student in an athletic program.

After this nightmare I stopped running for a long time. I still hung out with the guys on the team and several months later, the guys invited me to run in a 10K road race in Dallas. I had never run a 10K competitively. Without training I still finished 63rd out of over 1000 runners. All those previous miles under my belt likely helped me perform better than I expected. I ran in several more 10K road races, but only broke 35 minutes once.

During high school I worked at a few grocery stores. But the summer between high school and college I was looking for a summer job and read an ad for summer help in the classified section of the Dallas Times Herald. The job was with one of the United Van Lines moving companies in Dallas. They were hiring college students for the summer since this was the busy season for moving companies, so I applied – and got the job. The duties included loading and unloading furniture trucks and packing items in customers' homes prior to their move. The first summer I worked at this moving company, I met my best friend Brian, a student at Texas A&M, and we have been like brothers since.

The students were from various colleges throughout Texas. Each summer in college I returned to the same moving company along with the rest of the same students. Working in moving trucks in a Dallas summer was challenging enough, but the summer of 1980 had 42 consecutive days over 100 degrees—the hottest stretch over 100 degrees in Dallas history. That record still stands. What global warming? The summer of 1980 also included a total of 69 days over

100 degrees. Some weeks I worked between 50 and 60 hours. The heat inside these 18-wheeler trailers was well over 100 degrees and the work was hard, but it kept me in excellent shape. Then again, as a young adult of 18-22, you could leap over tall buildings in a single bound, fall out of planes, dust yourself off and keep going.

Eventually I moved into the office and worked as an assistant operations manager handling the paperwork of the moving crews and the dispatch. I worked each Saturday as the dispatch manager with a skeleton crew. Something my former boss in operations told me has helped me over the years. When there was too much going on and everything seemed to be falling apart, I kept asking him what I should do about this issue or that issue. He told me simply to "handle it." He was confident enough that I would analyze the options and make the right decision.

When I arrived at North Texas, I walked on the cross-country team running the 10K. Now I was in the big league, running against teams like Texas, Texas A&M and one of the best-known cross-country teams in the country, Arkansas. I couldn't compete at this level, nor did I have the motivation. We ran over 5 miles each morning before class and then again each evening. Saturday morning we ran around 10 miles and we had Sunday off. The team took the best seven runners to the weekly cross-country meet and twice I was the 7th runner for North Texas. Each team can have seven runners compete in the meets. In the last of these two meets I beat one of my teammates, but still I couldn't compete at this level. As I was closing in on the finish line of my first meet, I joked to myself that I hoped the officials had not yet turned the digital timer above the finish line off nor pulled up the cones. "Hey, you have another running coming in!" I later injured my knee and that was the beginning of the end of my running in college. Plus, in my first semester of my freshman year, I pledged a fraternity, Sigma Phi Epsilon (Sig Ep).

I could easily write a separate book on the mischief that took place at the Sig Ep house. This was the only fraternity house physically located on the North Texas campus. The other 15 or so fraternity houses were located off campus. We, however, were in the middle of the action. These were some of the best and most fun days of my youth. After my first semester in Clark Hall at North Texas I moved into the fraternity house and stayed until I graduated 4 years later. I've often joked that I would have stayed in this fraternity for an additional

10 years had my college funds not petered out.

My freshman year was busy. I was pledging to the fraternity and running cross-country. After I injured my knee, I knew I could not recover in time to continue the cross-country season. In high school I was able to compete with the best runners, but in college running 10K races was different and difficult for me to compete at a high level. So I quit the team. It was an easy decision.

The fraternity house was designed similar to a two-story motel. All of the 30 or so rooms faced outside, connected by walkways, and the house was L shaped. Each member residing in the house had their own room but shared a bathroom which connected the two rooms. We had a large party room with a bar. The party room was connected to our formal room for our weekly meetings. By no means was this a plush fraternity house. The rules... well, basically there were no rules. There was physical and mental hazing. There were drugs, though I never used or considered using them. There was no peer pressure. You weren't separated by drug user or no drug user. Everyone was cool and we really felt like brothers. In my Junior year, I was elected president of the fraternity. As I recall, I was the first president who didn't use drugs. Upon reflection, I suspect we were all pleased that in the early 80s there were no cell phone cameras. We couldn't have experienced the craziness that unfolded each day. The movie *Animal House*, released in 1978, painted a reasonably accurate picture of the activities inside our house. Loud and rowdy parties with beer and liquor bottles being thrown across the party room shattering on the walls. Numerous people passed out everywhere.

When we held pledge rush parties everyone was invited. Our parties were private, but aside from a silly theme party to which we could bring an unsuspecting date, the other parties were often paired with a sorority. The parties with sororities were called mixers. And all the parties revolved around a theme. We had toga, Caddyshack, red garter, bourbon street, rock star, Halloween, athletic supporters, spring and fall formal, Veterans' Day and many others. All these parties were held at our fraternity house. The Caddyshack mixers were the wildest. For the Caddyshack parties, the Alpha Phi sorority was our selected sorority. Their members were as deranged as our members. At the Caddyshack parties we were given a golf score card with an 18-hole course. This course was essentially 18 drink stations. Each station was set up on a different small table located in the party room. Like golf, after each round you would move to the next station. At each station there were various drinks. For example: a cup of beer, scotch and water, bourbon and coke, brandy, shot of whatever. Also like golf, each hole had a par which depended on how strong the drink was. The scotch and water might be a par 3, for example. If you drank this scotch and water with two sips, you birdied that hole. That may sound easy, but after several holes you were scoring bogeys and double bogeys or passing out.

Fraternity pledges were allowed to come to the parties, but they mostly worked the party. They ran each station and wrote down your score on the scorecard. I never made it past nine holes. At the end of the party, people were passed out all over the place. At one party, we learned that some of the girls passed out on campus, never making it all the way back to their dorms. At least most dorms were within sight of our fraternity house. And of course the pledges had to be at the fraternity house early the next morning to clean up the house.

It was difficult to study living in the fraternity house. Every day and night something was going on. The beer flowed 24 hours a day. It helped that we had two fraternity members who worked for Coors and Budweiser. All of this may have contributed to my grades being average.

At night we frequently had bottle rocket wars. Another member, now a doctor, and I used plastic golf club tubes with one opening taped closed to launch bottle rockets. Just light the fuse, drop the bottle rocket, aim the tube and it's on the way towards the victim. And it's very accurate. One night, in the middle of a bottle rocket war, the police arrived and one of our members was arrested in the yard of the fraternity house while the rest of us hid in our rooms. *Man down.*

I ran for president during my junior year, and after campaigning and making a speech at one of our formal meetings a vote was taken and I won the election. In a way it was like being the president of a company or a small country. I didn't realize how much work the president of a fraternity did. But being president taught me organization skills. I had to select fraternity members for various chairmen positions, attend University meetings, run fraternity meetings and meet with the higher ups in Clark Hall (located across the street from the fraternity house). I also had several meetings with the Assistant Dean of Students because some of our members bent a few campus rules. During my time living in the fraternity and my year as the president, when the police and fire department showed up it was because someone had called in a bomb scare. Most likely the *dormees* at Clark Hall. This became routine, so much so, that the nice firemen told us we had about five minutes to relocate anything in our rooms before they did their cursory bomb search.

I survived college and the fraternity, graduating with an average GPA, but I think I had a 4.0 in fraternity.

2

———◦·◦———

APPLYING TO BE AN FBI SPECIAL AGENT

It was during my early to middle teenage years when I began dreaming of becoming an FBI Special Agent (SA). I was inspired while watching the reruns of the series, "The Untouchables". The series ran from 1959 to 1963, with Robert Stack playing the lead character, Special Agent Eliot Ness, who was with the United States Department of the Treasury. Even though the series was not about the FBI, the series made me think about the FBI. I would sit on the floor in front of our 25-inch color TV and watch this black and white series and daydream. It was one of those dreams or fantasies that we have as a kid. "Oh, I'm going to be an astronaut, a fighter pilot, the President of the United States." My dream to be an FBI agent never left the back of my mind. I honestly didn't believe my ambition would come. But I was going to give it my best shot.

It was during my high school days that I heard my parents speak about my dad's dream of becoming an FBI agent. In fact, he had actually applied to the FBI, but soon discovered he wasn't qualified because he couldn't pass the initial eye examination. Your uncorrected vision could not be worse than 20-200. My dad failed the eye examination, which ended his dream of becoming an FBI agent. Many years later, we briefly talked about this. It wasn't until my application process in 1987 that we again discussed my dad's dream. My parents didn't believe I would be selected.

After I graduated with a degree in Finance from North Texas in

1984, I called the Dallas FBI office and asked about applying for an agent position. I spoke to the recruiter and was told that since I had graduated with a finance degree, I was required to wait a minimum of three years and acquire experience working in a professional field. After two and a half years I could apply and begin the process.

During this time I was working at United Van Lines as the Assistant Comptroller. It was a good job but not what I wanted to do. My boss was a great boss and friend, even today. He knew I was trying to become an FBI agent and would tease me and say it's not going to happen. One day my boss told me that an FBI agent, SA Lenny Becker* would be coming by the office on Saturday to pick up a few items out of storage, since he had just moved to the Dallas area. Since I was still opening the office on Saturdays with a skeleton crew, he asked me to take care of him. I was excited.

Sure enough that Saturday he came in and as he sat in the office signing some paperwork I said, "I'm sure you hear this a lot, but I really want to be an FBI agent. Can you give me some pointers?" SA Becker was cordial and spent time speaking to me about the job. For 31 years I did the same; I spoke to young kids who shared a similar dream. Jumping forward to around 1995, I was sitting at my desk on the White-Collar Crime Squad in the Memphis FBI office when I received a telephone call.

"This is SA Lenny Becker and, wow, you made it in the FBI," said the voice on the other end. "Do you remember me?"

I said, "Absolutely," then thanked him before exchanging stories. Jumping forward again, to around 2008, I was sitting at my desk in the Counter Terrorism Squad in the Dallas FBI office and reading an FBI document when I saw SA Lenny Becker's name. He was in Washington, DC. I immediately sent him an email about how much I love my job and how he was such an inspiration. He responded and said that he told his wife about my sincere and passionate comments and that she had teared up. He was getting close to retirement.

I submitted my agent application two and half years after I graduated. After submitting my application, I had to take the same eye examination my dad had failed several years before. I knew my eyesight was on the edge of the standard and worried I might fail the same as my dad. This was not a test you could pull an all-nighter studying for. By a slim margin I passed and was on my way. I was told that I fell into the category: white male diversified. At the time, the FBI was hiring individuals with accounting or law degrees and if you held other degrees, you fell into the diversified category. You were given less preference and less of a chance of being selected. I was also told that being a white male reduced my chances.

I didn't fully understand what my chances were until one day at the FBI academy, someone came into our classroom and began writing information and numbers on the chalkboard. Applicants were given extra points for being in the military, holding a law or accounting degree or being a minority or female. This individual explained the point system and how it affected the applicants' scores. We were told that all FBI academy classes must have eight women, no matter what. After this person left, the classroom was silent for several seconds and one of the women in the classroom said something to the effect that this was bullshit, and she had earned the right to be at the FBI academy. I didn't see a need for this person to present this information to the class. What was the point and what good did it do? We had eight and lost one early after failing a test twice. I had to assume this person had gone to the other agent academy classes and shared the same information. But now I realized how difficult my ride through the selection process was. That said, I can confirm from experience that we have excellent female and minority agents in the FBI, and I was proud to work with each and every one.

Several years after I was selected (the word "selected" is correct. It would drive me crazy when someone would say "join" the FBI. You "join" a country club or a sewing group), I learned that only approximately 4 percent of all applicants are selected. I was on the other side of the table for 23 years interviewing agent applicants and the trend continued to be true.

After filling out an application and submitting it to the Dallas FBI office, I received a call to come in for a written test. I learned that approximately 50 percent pass this test. I passed and hoped to receive a call to come in for an interview. Sometime later I did receive this call. I knew the interview would be conducted by three agents and would mostly cover global current events. Even though I was nervous, I was confident since I was well-versed in news of the world. Since I was a young teenager I had read the newspaper daily, and not just the sports section. I was interested in world events. As I sat in the lobby, I recall how nervous I was just staring into space.

This reminds me of a time when I was on the other side of the interview table interviewing agent applicants. I was in Santa Monica, California at one of my usual destinations for a week of interviewing applicants (Phase II, later described in the book) who were mostly from the west coast. I had just returned from my favorite breakfast diner a few blocks from the Santa Monica hotel we stayed in and conducted the applicant interviews. I was sitting in the small hotel lobby dressed in shorts and a tee shirt, relaxing before I needed to go upstairs, shower, dress and head to the floor where these interviews would be conducted.

As I sat on the hotel lobby couch, no one was around except a young man dressed in slacks and a starched white dress shirt. I was pretty sure he was an FBI agent applicant waiting for his interview. He was pacing while holding a tie in his hand. He looked at me, hesitated then walked over to me and asked, "Sir do you know how to tie a tie?" His uncertainty was probably prompted by my current state of dress. I told him that I did. I tie an excellent tie - ties should end in a small knot, not like those worn in the 1970s. I stood up, tied the tie around my neck, pulled it off and put it around his neck. I pulled the tie up for a perfect look. He thanked me several times and I wished him good luck, then I went upstairs and got ready.

As I walked on the floor toward the interview rooms dressed in my sharp, expensive Lombardo Custom Apparel suit, the applicants were lined up with their backs against the wall near the interview rooms. There he was. Our eyes fixed on each other and his facial expression changed to a surprised look. I slowed my walk as I began to pass him, turned toward him, nodded slightly and said "Good luck" again. I can't imagine what he thought. "This guy who was earlier dressed in shorts and a tee shirt and tied my tie was an FBI agent?" I don't know if he passed or failed. I hoped he passed. I'm sure I had that same nervous look while I waited, with my perfectly tied tie, in the Dallas FBI office lobby for my future to begin. Incidentally, I met Al Pacino that day. He was in a small conference room next to ours. He was very congenial, and we had a short conversation.

I wore various pieces of Lombardo apparel during some of my rich guy undercover roles. Lombardo Custom Apparel is located in a Dallas suburb and owned by a very good friend, Jay Lombardo. We were in the Sig Ep fraternity together at the University of North Texas and after we graduated we both had very successful careers. Lombardo's creates excellent custom-made clothes. Yes, the clothes are pricey, but so is a McLaren. Many of their customers are celebrities—Dallas Cowboys (several hall of famers), Dallas Mavericks, and other professional sports players throughout the country. And, of course, my all-time favorite, Tony Romo.

My agent interview, unlike today's agent interviews, was a much more laid-back atmosphere. I'll later touch on today's interview process, since I was on the other side of that table for 23 years. After my interview concluded, I felt good about it. Then again, maybe I bombed. You never know. Yet I'll never forget how one of the agents who interviewed me, SA Hector Garza* put his arm on my shoulder as he walked me out of the office and told me I was one of the best applicants he had ever interviewed. He gave me his number and we stayed in touch.

Weeks later, I received a letter from the FBI and nervously opened it. A short letter included mention of my score of 89 in the interview. What did that mean? An 89 has to be a great score, right? Weeks later, I received another letter from the FBI and I began to open it. Did my dream come true? As I type this, I am reminded of scenes in the outstanding movie *Rudy* when Rudy kept opening letters from the University of Notre Dame to see if he was accepted. Just like Rudy, the answer in the letter was no. But we also know that later Rudy did receive a letter of acceptance. My letter stated that I wasn't competitive enough at this time. How could that be? I scored an 89.

I sat down on the floor in my apartment and worried that my dream was over. What was I going to do? I called SA Garza and he was surprised and disappointed. I asked what I could do. "Do I need to go back to college and earn an accounting degree?" He answered, "Just wait. I'll will find out what happened."

Months later I learned that my applicant process was moving forward, years later I learned why. My background investigation had begun, and the agent conducting the background investigation was knocking on doors in my parents' neighborhood and also speaking with friends. The agent conducting my background investigation called me one day and asked the name of my Dallas Times Herald paper route manager. I couldn't believe that he was going to interview this person. I was only 13 years old when I delivered papers. I was surprised that I remembered his name and provided it to the agent.

In 1988, to be hired as an agent it was imperative that you had no prior drug use. Not even if you tried it once. Several years ago, that sadly changed. I had no worries, since I never tried drugs nor even tried a cigarette. I wasn't concerned or worried that the FBI would conduct a background check at my old fraternity house. Of course, they did. I later learned that some Sig Ep members were sitting on the front porch of the fraternity house in 1988 when an FBI agent showed up and began asking about me. These members probably wondered what Kamel had done to bring the FBI to our fraternity house. They knew of me from stories they'd heard and knew that I was once the president of the fraternity. They even showed the agent an old photo of the fraternity members including myself with the title of "President" under my picture.

A month or so later I received a call from the Dallas FBI office informing me that an agent would be arriving at my office to interview employees at United Van Lines as part of my background investigation. Only my boss knew that I had applied to the FBI and that the process had reached this far. There were a lot of surprised co-workers. A short time later the Dallas office called and told me that I had been selected for new agents' academy class 88-13, beginning 9/6/1988. I had just a few weeks to report. Like Rudy, I had finally received my "yes."

A short time after I transferred to the Dallas office, SA Garza was retired and he invited me to lunch. He told me that the FBI letter that initially denied my selection for the new agents class was incorrect. He had spoken to the recruiter and asked why I wasn't selected with the high score I had received. They reviewed the applicant paperwork, which was completed after the interview score, and learned that one box was incorrectly checked. This is what had paused my selection. The recruiter was pleased that SA Garza inquired about this, and the paperwork was corrected. I was happily surprised when SA Garza explained this mix-up to me.

My dad's dream of becoming an FBI agent did not really come full circle until a year after I retired. I was cleaning out closets at my mom's residence and I came across a box containing old photographs and letters my dad had tucked away. My mom and I sat and looked through these old photographs and I came across letters that my dad had written to my mom while they were dating. I asked my mom if I could read these letters to her and she said yes. The words and phrases they used in the 1950s were corny. Things like "my darling" and "sweetheart". But one of my dad's letters to my mom caught my attention. In the letter, he revealed that he planned to become an FBI agent and then flirted with my mom about how he was preparing for that role. Now I understand how truly proud my dad was of me. I guess he lived his dream through me.

3

NEW AGENTS ACADEMY CLASS

When I left for the academy, it was difficult for my parents. Until my departure, none of the kids had left Dallas. I entered the FBI academy just after I turned 27, which was young compared to the average age at the time of 29 to 30 years old. I had lived a sheltered life. I'd only traveled to seven surrounding states, so I was a little overwhelmed after I flew into Washington DC and rode the shuttle bus to the FBI academy. I was nervous, but also excited and I wasn't going to let myself down. I had no legal or law enforcement background. I had very little knowledge of a grand jury's role and had no knowledge of what a Federal Magistrate did. I had never fired a handgun—just a shotgun, and a .22 rifle a few times. At the FBI academy back then, from day one to graduation was approximately 14 weeks. Today the academy is over 20 weeks long.

At the academy, we trained and qualified with a .357 revolver, which had a .38 plus P round. The very first day at the FBI academy range, a firearms instructor was walking up and down the line. He stopped and asked me if I had ever shot a handgun and I responded "No." He said I would be one of his favorite students. I didn't know how to take that. Was that a positive or a negative? He further explained that the FBI could train me without worrying about breaking bad firearms habits I might have developed. I was fresh. For many reasons, I did not like the .357. A weapon with a six round capacity is outdated for today's law enforcement and was even back in 1988. Plus, the FBI issued agents a "speed loader" with this weapon. This plastic device carried six rounds but by no means had any speed to it, no matter how fast you were. It was notably slow compared to the speed I was able to achieve changing magazines in any one of my later semi-automatic handguns. At the academy, we also trained with the 12-gauge pump action shotgun using both a slug round and 9 shot buckshot round, with a five-round capacity.

There were three areas that an agent needed to excel in at the academy: academics, firearms and physical fitness. I excelled in physical fitness. Academics was the one area that really tested me. At the FBI academy they had a place called the "board room" where you could order food and beer and relax. I didn't go to the board room until the last week of the academy. On a few occasions, when some of my classmates were heading to the board room they would stop by my room and ask me to join them. I was in my room studying, unlike college.

"Why are you studying now, the next test isn't for another week?" they'd ask. One of the classmates was a WestPoint graduate. I thought, *does he really need to study?* I reiterated that I needed to study. And I did. At the academy if you failed the same test twice you were out. Pack your bags don't let the door hit you in the ass. Anything below 85 on an exam was a failing grade. An 84 was failing? I would have been pretty excited about those grades in college. Frankly, I didn't study in college unless I was really concentrating on which costume to select for a themed frat party. If I received an 85 or 90 in college, I always just assumed there was a curve. I certainly didn't earn that because of studying. But I didn't want to fail the academy and my dream, simply because I didn't give maximum effort. There was only one close call: on a legal exam I scored an 85.

Approximately eight or ten other classmates scored below an 85, including my roommate. The class counselor announced that the second exam for these classmates was scheduled for the coming Friday. They had just a few days to study. Someone in the class stood up and asked the counselor if they could take the test the following Monday instead, so they could have the weekend to study. Without hesitation the counselor said, "No, we will have the exam Friday, so if anyone fails they will have the weekend to pack and leave the academy." This was an eye opener.

The test was held on a Friday morning. That afternoon I heard the back door to the classroom open and, like my classmates, turned around to see who was interrupting the class. Two class counselors walked up to one of the students and whispered something in her ear. She cleared off her desk, stood up and walked out of the classroom with the counselors. She had failed the second legal exam. Another eye opener.

I did well in fitness and firearms. One of the fitness requirements was that we had to run a timed two miles on the track during the first week of the academy. This was right up my alley. We also had to run this timed two miles again several weeks later and then one more time before we graduated. The first time I finished a very close second. I couldn't believe someone beat me. The second time I barely finished first, ahead of the same classmate. On the last run we tied for first.

We heard from students in prior FBI agent academy classes that we would be trained with CS gas. The training would include being gassed inside an enclosed school bus. These students made it sound like a nightmare. While on the FBI academy campus I often walked by this school bus sitting in a parking lot, not knowing when that day would come. I think the school bus was always smiling.

I understood the purpose of the training, which was to introduce agents to the effects of CS gas. The gas training day finally came. We first had classroom training, which included how to quickly and correctly don your gas masks. On the day of training, we were told to wear clothes we might need to discard and meet by the school bus with our gas masks. One of the instructions we were given was very confusing. An instructor told us that after being gassed and exiting the bus, we were to use the water they had available to rinse the CS gas out of our eyes. Another instructor told us not to use the water because it would saturate the CS gas into our eyes and pores. I decided to go the water route.

The bus windows were closed. Standing next to the school bus we were told to don our masks, enter the bus, find a seat and sit down. Logic would tell you to sit as close to the front of the bus as possible, so that you could be the first off the bus once the torture began. The instructors were too smart for this. I sat somewhere in the middle.

A few instructors wearing gas masks entered the bus. They released the gas, and the misery began. We were told to remove our gas masks and remain seated until an instructor tapped your shoulder. Once tapped you could exit the bus. Sitting near the front wasn't an advantage at all. If you panicked and exited the bus before being tapped, you would have to repeat the training. There was so much gas in the bus I could barely see a few feet in front of me. *How nice. Maybe I'll just sit here and order a cup of coffee.* After what seemed like a lifetime, an instructor stood up and walked down the aisle and randomly tapped the victims on their shoulders, allowing them to exit. Naturally the instructor walked past me and selected others to exit the bus first. Finally I felt the tap and I walked off the bus, acting as though all was well in my world. But, after getting outside and drenching myself with water, the gas really began to kick my butt. After several hours, I fully recovered. Rumor had it that our Kevlar bulletproof vests would be tested...while we wore the vests. But that rumor turned out to be a tall tale.

If you haven't heard of Hogan's Alley at the FBI academy, I suggest you look it up. Hogan's Alley was opened in 1987, just in time for me to enjoy the town. Even in 1988, it was, and still is impressive. It is literally a fake, but realistic small town. You have a bank, movie theater (named Biograph Theater - where John Dillinger was shot and killed by FBI agents in Chicago), pool hall, laundromat, hotel, apartments, post office, and other shops. The town stays active with FBI staff and is located on the FBI academy campus. Hogan's Alley is used as a training site for various arrest scenarios. As you walk up to the perimeter there is a warning sign that advises that there are ongoing law enforcement arrest scenarios and you could be subject to these activities. When these training arrest scenarios are ongoing, actors and actresses are portraying subjects, victims and witnesses. These actors and actresses play their parts as realistically as they can. There are chases, people being tackled and wrestled to the ground, weapons firing paintballs and much more.

On one occasion during training I was the lead arresting agent. I had a few minutes to address my small team with limited information on the subject we had an outstanding arrest warrant for. The instructors told me that the subject was last seen in the pool hall. As I assembled my team, I placed two agents at the front entrance, in case the subject tried to flee, and I had two agents accompany me inside. As I walked in, I was astonished. This small pool hall was as real as it gets, complete with dimly lit bar, people playing pool and drinking at the bar, loud music and clouds of cigarette smoke. People were moving around as if I had just walked into a real pool hall. Within a minute, two guys playing pool looked up at us; one immediately ran through the small crowd and out the back door. The three of us were in pursuit.

I yelled "FBI" and grabbed him, surprised by how hard he fought me. It took three of us to tackle him. I couldn't believe a real fight was going on. After we subdued him and began questioning him, the instructors stopped the arrest exercise and asked me why I arrested him. I incorrectly told the instructor that he ran, so we chased him. The instructor said, "The guy you are holding is not your subject." Oops. We had reacted like a dog chasing a rabbit. Still, the instructor gave me credit for leaving the two agents up front and as the real subject walked out the front door, they arrested him. It wasn't a total loss, but it sure was a good training lesson.

Approximately three quarters through the FBI academy they tell you where the FBI will send you. And if it's not one of the major FBI offices, you will be transferred no later than four years later to a major office. That changed after I had been an agent for three and a half years. Dallas was a major office. Years later they allowed you to list your top 10 choices. For my class I think they put up a large map of the United States and threw a dart at it and that is where they were assigning you. The day we learned which FBI office we were being assigned to we were called up to the front of the class with a United States map hanging behind us. The class counselor handed you an envelope. You opened the envelope in front of your classmates and read to the class where you were being assigned. I opened mine and the dart hit on Memphis. For me that wasn't bad, since it was closer to home than numerous other possible locations. The cost of living was also affordable like Texas, with no state income taxes. At graduation I was given my FBI credentials and badge and I collected my newly assigned .357 revolver at the gun vault. I would be boarding my first plane with my firearm on my side soon thereafter. I loved the Memphis FBI office, but not the city.

Out of Quantico, new agents were assigned a particular brand, model number and round for the weapon. During my career the FBI only allowed a very short list of weapons and model numbers that agents were allowed to carry. If you carried an authorized secondary weapon, one not assigned by the FBI, you had to purchase the weapon through an approved vendor and the weapon must be first sent to the firearms unit at the FBI academy in Quantico. Once the firearms unit processed the weapon, the weapon was then sent to the principal firearms instructor in that division. An agent must also qualify with the secondary weapon or any weapon the agent is authorized to carry.

During my career, the FBI changed approved weapons numerous times. These included the .357 (revolver), 10mm, .40 caliber and various 9mm handguns. After you were assigned to a division, Agents were required to qualify with their assigned weapons four times per year. Agents needed a minimum score of 80 out of 100 to pass, based on a timed 50 round course utilizing a silhouetted target.

This changed slightly for me in 1990. I was in the Memphis Division, standing at the urinal, when one of the SWAT team leaders asked if I would be interested in trying out for the SWAT team. He said he based this on my fitness, shooting skill and character. What is that saying – opportunities arise at opportune times? At the time, I wasn't thinking about the SWAT team, I had barely been an agent for two years, but the possibility was intriguing.

I made the team. The SWAT team is considered collateral duty and you are still expected to maintain your investigative case load. SWAT team members don't receive extra pay even though the risk is higher. This is the way it should be.

On the SWAT team, we did weapons qualification more frequently. We used a smaller silhouetted target and our allotted qualifying course time was shorter and more rigorous. We were required to shoot a minimum score of 90 out of 100 to pass. The qualifying distance ranged from 3 yards to 25 yards with the handguns. Most of the course required you to pull from the holster to engage the target. The targets are bladed until you hear the fire command, then the target quickly turns and faces you for the time period you are allocated at each firing distance. Then the target will quickly flip back to its bladed position. For example, from the five-yard line you are facing a bladed target with your hands in front of your body (in the ready position). Your weapon is covered by a shirt or jacket and once the target turns, you quickly have to push your shirt or jacket back, pull your weapon and fire two shots in three seconds before your target turns back to its bladed position. Any slight mishandling of your shirt or jacket or pulling your weapon and there's little chance of getting two shots off in time, let alone on target. The holster I carried, and still carry, doesn't have a "thumb break." I was able to jerk my weapon immediately and cleanly from my holster without having to deal with a mechanism holding the weapon down in my holster. Some of our FBI firearm instructors weren't pleased with me using this type of holster, but I was more offensive than defensive. You had to be quick to draw, as well as an accurate shot to hit your target like a top quarterback.

While I'm talking about holsters, I'll add that I'm against the ankle holster. I'm not saying that I haven't used them, but only rarely. Most unexpected confrontations occur quickly. One or two seconds can mean the difference between life and death. I'm not talking about going out on a planned arrest, whereas you are prepared for a confrontation. I'm referring to everyday life. When an immediate confrontation occurs, what are you going to do? Call time out so you can reach down and pull out your weapon? It takes more time and movement to reach and pull from an ankle holster. If you pulled from your ankle holster and I pulled from my side holster, I'd win 100 percent of the time. This is not a sports event. This is life or death.

In 1998, after transferring to the FBI Dallas Division, I had the opportunity to join the Dallas FBI SWAT team, but I first needed to prove myself. The Dallas team was understandably larger with much more activity including more higher risk arrests. A few years later, the FBI SWAT teams were allowed to carry a special FBI Springfield model 1910 .45, which was enhanced at the FBI firearms unit. The .45 was a bigger and heavier weapon, but more powerful than the 9mm, 10mm and .40 weapons we had previously been assigned. Naturally the weapon carried fewer rounds; eight plus one. Prior to carrying the .45, most of our weapons had a capacity of 15 plus one.

Unlike what you see in movies and TV shows portraying FBI agents, your weapon also has a round in the chamber and there is no safety to flip on or off. Also unlike the movies and TV shows, you were trained never to have your finger on the trigger unless you intended to fire the weapon. I'm amazed when watching these movies and TV shows to see the actor or actress running around with their weapons out and their finger on the trigger. So many terrible things could go wrong, from a reflex or a stumble. Also, there are no warning shots, no aiming for a limb and no shooting out tires to disable a vehicle. When you place your figure on the trigger you are intending to fire your weapon to stop an adversary with deadly force. You also don't fire your weapon just once. The SWAT teams were allowed to carry the .45 but were required to conduct rigorous training to qualify with the weapon, including combat courses. Each of our .45s had a unique number not only engraved on the weapon, but also on the various parts of the weapon. So when you noticed agents throughout the country carrying the .45, you knew they were members of the FBI SWAT team. It was definitely the sexiest handgun in the FBI. I guess it would be like the paratroopers in WW2 who earned their "jump wings."

My thoughts about this weapon were shared by a number of other FBI SWAT team members throughout the country. More parts and not as easy to clean. The weapon was definitely a showstopper. My accuracy was better with the .45. It was the most accurate handgun I carried with the FBI… *when it fired*. The jam rate on these .45s was higher, which was concerning. When you need to fire your weapon at an adversary you want to be able to count on it working. It's that simple. It's similar to a parachute—when you need the parachute to open you need it to open.

After we trained and qualified with the .45, we carried it as a daily weapon. Some members of the SWAT team who were equally concerned with the higher jam rate of their .45 chose to go back to the regular assigned FBI weapons like the .40 caliber. Over time, I noticed several members chose not to carry the .45 as an everyday weapon, not even on SWAT missions. I was one of the last holdouts to trade my .45 in. But that happened quite by accident. The principal firearms instructor, who was also on the SWAT team, told me it was time for my .45 to be sent to the firearms unit at Quantico for maintenance. I was given a loaner weapon (not a .45). Several weeks later, the firearms instructor advised me that my .45 was back and I could come pick it up. I told him I was no longer interested in carrying the .45. Besides the unpredictable jamming, the gun was prone to tear many suit jackets.

Other weapons we carried were the pump 12-gauge shotgun (in my early days as an agent), which had a shorter barrel. I didn't like this weapon and can't really explain why. You either loaded five rounds of nine-shot buckshot or five rounds of slug in the weapon. You wouldn't want to be hit with the slug round. The shotgun was our only long weapon in my early days. Early in my career when I was on the Memphis SWAT team we carried the MP5 9mm then as time evolved, after arriving in the Dallas Division, I carried the MP5 10mm fully automatic (only for SWAT team members). This MP5 had a safety, one shot, two shot and fully automatic fire modes. We always used the two-shot fire mode. There was no real need to flip the lever to the fully automatic mode. But it was fun to use. I learned how to hold the weapon in a different manner and with one pull of the trigger I could put all 30 rounds in the target. This became my favorite weapon. I always could get the weapon in action quickly. It had a nice and easy-to-use collapsible stock. Also, I was able to obtain a tight grouping of my shots on a target. I felt like I could pick and hit buttons on someone's shirt with this weapon. During my last few years on the Dallas SWAT team we changed from the MP5 (I think I was the last holdout) to a tactical M4 carbine. Most of the new SWAT team members loved this weapon. It was definitely a more powerful weapon, but I'll take the MP5.

4

---·◦·---

COMPLAINT DUTY AND WEEKLY DUTY

Each FBI Division might have a slightly different policy in handling agents being called out after regular work hours and on weekends. Memphis and Dallas are generally the same, it's just that more manpower is required in a larger division like Dallas. While I was assigned to the Memphis Division, we had "weekly duty." All FBI Headquarter offices are open 24 hours a day, 7 days a week. Resident Agency (RA) offices, which are satellite FBI offices within divisions and could have as few as two agents, have more limited hours. In Memphis, during this time period, one agent was required to respond to any after-hours call. This meant between 5:00 PM and the following morning at 8:15 AM and also included the beginning of Friday at 5:00 PM through Monday, 8:15 AM. Your response time was generally immediate depending on the circumstances. You might be able to solve the problem with a few phone calls or you might need to respond to the issue in person. It's important to note that if you were responding in person, you would call a second agent to help out. In my experience, 99 percent of the time the agent you were calling would jump right in unless they were out of town or had a previous engagement that truly prevented them from assisting. I usually called an agent who I had worked with and was a friend. Likewise, I was expected to help if this same agent called me at 2:00 AM asking for my assistance. This weekly duty was rotated amongst all street agents. [Note: Street agents are basically agents involved in case investigations and undercover work, compared to Supervisory Special Agents (SSA), upper management agents and the few agents not assigned to casework.]

In Memphis your lucky straw came up about once every five or six months. If your name appeared during a time period you planned to be on leave, locally or out of town, it was your responsibility to change your schedule or switch with another willing agent. Usually this wasn't a problem. But it was important to make clear arrangements head of time. If a call came in at 2:00 AM to the Memphis Headquarters, the support employee would need to know the agent on call for that week. And—ring-ring—that's when you'd receive the call at home. Agents didn't have cell phones back in the dark ages of 1991. The policies in Memphis and Dallas were generally the same. In Dallas, a much larger FBI Division, we had as many as five agents from various squads on call during weekly duty. For most occasions, one agent could handle the call unless it required you to mobilize to a location.

In addition to weekly duty, each FBI office had "complaint duty" assigned to at least one agent, depending on the size of the division. This is a one-day assignment. Several years prior to my retirement this was essentially eliminated, but while it was in effect, complaint duty required the agent to remain in the FBI office during regular work hours of 8:15 AM to 5:00 PM to handle complaint calls or "walk-ins." A call would come into the division's main number and if the support employee deemed it necessary, the support employee would contact the agent assigned to the complaint duty and transfer that call back to the agent to handle. Prior to the call being transferred, however, the support employee would give a summary of the complaint. Based on the information received from the complainant, the agent wrote up the information the complainant provided and this information was entered into the FBI database. An SSA would review the information to determine if further investigation was warranted. But, even prior to the SSA review, an experienced agent could determine if further investigation was needed. On many occasions, the agent could offer advice to the complainant, especially when the complaint call didn't meet FBI jurisdiction or other thresholds, which could result in an FBI investigation. In my experience, at least 75 percent of these calls could be handled during the telephone conversation. These included domestic problems, civil matters or matters handled by the local police or even another federal agency. I would provide the caller with the agency or department that would or could handle these issues. Other times these matters could be handled by a private attorney, unless there were Federal violations.

The priorities handed down by FBI headquarters in Washington play a major role in determining the opening of an investigation. For more than half my career, the priorities fell under white-collar crime. That all changed drastically after 9/11. But even in white-collar crime, there were priorities for each type of violation. If the complaint alleged fraud, and the loss was under the division's monetary threshold, the FBI division would not open an investigation. I always asked the complainant if this was an actual loss or potential loss. Potential loss versus actual loss also carried weight in determining if a case would be opened. The Memphis and Dallas divisions wouldn't open an investigation based on an amount of expected loss or actual loss immensely under the thresholds set by the respective offices. While I was assigned to the Memphis division white-collar crime squad, the loss threshold hovered around half that of the Dallas division's threshold, though these numbers weren't hard and fast rules—other factors also played a part in determining the opening of a case.

Regardless, I would write up the information and search the FBI databases, utilizing the name(s) of the alleged subject(s) to determine if there were other victim complaints about the alleged fraud scheme. If in fact there were other complaints/victims of fraud by the same subject(s), that information could influence the opening an investigation. The FBI database searches sometimes resulted in the discovery of another division with an open investigation on the alleged subject(s). If, after an FBI database search, the agent learned that another FBI division had an open investigation on this subject(s), this information would be shared with the other division. I received information on numerous occasions from other divisions for an open case I was investigating. After contacting the victim located in the other FBI division, I would add the relevant details to my open case.

5

INTERVIEWS, GUILTY PLEAS AND
INDICTMENTS

I always conducted the interviews for my subject and my potential subjects. I would also have a second agent with me to assist in the interviews, even if the subject was located in another division. If the subject cooperated and admitted to the federal violations, I would advise the prosecutor, an Assistant United States Attorney (AUSA).

For witness and victim interviews located in other divisions, you are expected to send leads to the other divisions to interview the witnesses and victims. I don't recall ever having an SSA deny my travel to another FBI division to conduct a subject or potential subject interview. This was a huge benefit for my investigations. If instead, the case agent sent a lead to another division to conduct a subject interview in a complex white-collar crime case, the interview would be difficult for the agent in that division and the results wouldn't be as beneficial. The agent covering the lead had limited knowledge of the case and very little leverage.

When I traveled to another FBI Division to interview a subject or potential subject, I knew my case backward and forward. I had strong evidence against the subject, whereas if the subject didn't cooperate, my case was still ready for indictment. So, before I approached the subject, I gathered more than enough evidence to indict the subject. I preferred to obtain the subject's admission to his or her guilt in an interview. Besides the overwhelming evidence, I used my experience and resourcefulness to obtain a subject's admission. One of the keys to this success is that I always showed up unannounced for a "cold call" interview. There was always a second agent with me for safety reasons and for a second witness. If the subject decided to admit to his or her guilt, then the indictment process and an early morning visit by several agents to the subject's home would be unnecessary.

White-collar crime subjects usually preferred to avoid the unwanted attention they would receive in their neighborhood when numerous agents wearing FBI raid jackets arrived at their door. Agents and AUSAs preferred to avoid trial, which would occur if the subject admitted to their guilt. Also, many subjects preferred to avoid trial for cost reasons and if they lost in trial they would receive a longer sentence. Some simply preferred to avoid having their name in the news. "A good agent does not go to trial." Almost all of my subjects in White-collar Crime cases pled guilty either to an "information" or after they were indicted.

The "information" is a way for the subject to agree to plead guilty instead of being indicted by a Grand Jury. There were several subjects in my cases that would not plead guilty until after they were indicted. The Grand Jury indictments in my cases were 100 percent, which probably isn't as impressive as it sounds, since the indictment probability in FBI cases throughout the country is close to 99 percent. When I had to take my case to the Grand Jury for indictment, the subjects hired an Attorney, but eventually realized that it was better to plead guilty instead of playing a losing hand in trial. If they decided to plead guilty prior to the indictment, they would plead to an "information" and later plead guilty before the Federal Judge. Only a few of my subjects went to trial and when they did they were convicted. I credit this to my thorough investigation and the overwhelming evidence I obtained.

For almost all my cases I was the sole case agent. I enjoyed the fact that I was the sole decision maker about the direction of the case, what steps I wanted to take and when.

FBI agents use various tools to further their investigation. A common tool is the subpoena for records. I can't think of a case where I didn't use at least one subpoena to obtain records. For example, a subpoena request for records on someone's bank account is a very simple process of contacting the AUSA in your case, and providing the name of the bank, the name registered to the account and account number. Another common tool was the search warrant, which I can proudly say I never used. The search warrant request is a lot more work compared to the subpoena. I never saw a need for a search warrant. I was able to obtain enough evidence through subpoenas, interviews and other methods to convict the subject(s). I have been part of many search warrants where hundreds and hundreds of boxes filled with seized documents were placed in evidence. All for the case agent to spend endless hours reviewing. Many of these search warrants were requested by less experienced agents. It always seemed like overkill. Search warrants required a great deal of manpower and resources. My standing rule was: if you don't need to use this tool, don't.

MEMPHIS DIVISION

6

—◦•◦—

YOU'RE OUR GUY

When I graduated from the FBI academy in December 1988, I was assigned to the white-collar crime squad in the Memphis office. When I was at the FBI academy, we were told that if you could successfully investigate white-collar crime you would be able to handle any other FBI cases, since white-collar crime cases were the most complex. A less-difficult case could easily take longer than a year, but mine averaged three-plus years. Of course, most agents have more than one active open case and maybe as many as ten. Also, agents had collateral duties, such as being assigned to cover leads from other FBI divisions or numerous other events that required agents to respond. I stayed on that squad for the entire nine and a half years in Memphis.

While in Memphis, I enjoyed working with the members of the white-collar crime squad and the SSA. Our office was very laid back. When I first arrived the FBI office was in downtown Memphis, but it later moved east to within seven minutes from my house. Even better, our firearms training and qualifying range was between my house and the office. What luck.

After only working in the Memphis office for about a year I was assigned a lead from the Chicago FBI division. Even though the squad I was assigned to was a white-collar crime squad, we were also assigned fugitive cases. Normally the fugitive cases were assigned to the violent crime squads, but our squad was happy to have them. These cases added a little change of pace from our complex, white-collar crime cases. In fugitive cases, the subjects have outstanding federal warrants for various crimes. For example, if an individual had a warrant for murder and the local authorities had the slightest belief that the subject had fled the jurisdiction, perhaps to another state, an Unlawful Flight to Avoid Prosecution (UFAP) warrant would be issued. Since the FBI's jurisdiction covered the entire United States and its territories, the FBI had authority to apprehend these individuals. If they fled the United States, we would enter their information into Interpol. Interpol is the International Police Organization, with almost 200 countries participating. Subjects could be picked up in any of these countries. I had success with the arrest of two subjects using Interpol. One was arrested in New Delhi, India, and the other was on a flight manifest traveling from Nigeria to Houston.

The lead from Chicago was for the Memphis office to locate and arrest a UFAP, Cedric Jenner*, who had been wanted for over 17 years in connection with violent crimes in the Chicago area. The Chicago case agent had compelling evidence that Jenner was living under an assumed name, Cedric Smith*, and was at a particular address with his family. It was likely that Jenner's family didn't know Jenner's true identity, nor that he was wanted by the FBI, since he married after becoming a fugitive and used the name Smith. The Chicago lead was to arrest Jenner if in fact the information the Chicago case agent provided was correct. Jenner would then face charges in Chicago.

Since I was new, I asked the SWAT team leader, SA Ethan Youngblood*, who was assigned to the violent crime squad, to assist. I showed him the information provided in the lead, which included old photographs, an arrest history and several identifiers including Jenner's fingerprint classification. SA Youngblood was experienced in these types of matters and eager to assist. I didn't know SA Youngblood very well, but he had a good reputation on the violent crime squad. Once I made the Memphis SWAT team, we became good friends.

We put together a small team. I carried Jenner's old photographs and other relevant information to be used in this potential arrest. I arrived at the residence with the rest of the team in the middle of the day. With other agents surrounding the residence, SA Youngblood and I knocked on the front door and bladed ourselves toward the door. A man who appeared to look like Jenner answered the knock on the door. His wife and kids were standing near the doorway. We identified ourselves and told him to step outside. I said, "You're Jenner, wanted in Chicago 17 years ago." He stepped outside and denied being Jenner and said his name was Smith. He produced identification showing him as Cedric Smith. He didn't display any hostility. We stayed on alert anyway while the other agents had their weapons drawn, covering us. SA Youngblood then grabbed Jenner's hand, turned it over and closely looked at his fingertips. Then SA Youngblood said, "You are our guy," and we cuffed Jenner. At that point, Jenner admitted to being the fugitive wanted over 17 years ago. He asked to speak to his family first; we allowed him a few minutes. Jenner's family was understandably in shock.

After we had Jenner in custody, I pulled one of the agents aside and said I was impressed with SA Youngblood's bluff about the fingerprints. The agent explained to me that this wasn't a bluff. In fact, prior to becoming an agent, SA Youngblood worked in the FBI fingerprint section. He knew exactly what he was looking for.

Later, I thanked SA Youngblood and told him I'd thought he'd been bluffing. He confirmed that it was not a bluff. Prior to the arrest, SA Youngblood had reviewed Jenner's criminal history, which included Jenner's fingerprint classification. SA Youngblood explained that he was able to look at enough loops and whorls on Jenner's fingertips to know we had the fugitive. Still, I was very impressed with SA Youngblood and the FBI.

7

---·◦·◦·---

THE FIRST KIDNAPPING

I was on weekly duty during a typical early summer weekend in 1991. You know, yard work, small house projects, grilling out back, enjoying the pool. But this weekend was different. I could not have imagined that I would be flying to Las Vegas early Sunday morning, returning a kidnapped 21-month-old little girl.

That Saturday morning I was doing my usual work around the house when the Memphis FBI office called. I was told that the Las Vegas FBI office requested immediate assistance from our office to cover a few leads located in the Memphis Area of Operation (AO). Immediate lead details would follow. The Memphis support employee provided me with the name and contact information for the Las Vegas FBI case agent. Of course, in 1991 we weren't operating with cell phones, but with pagers. The pager would give you a number to call and most of the time if you felt it was important you looked for a payphone or another land line phone to make that call.

I had the Memphis office patch me through to the Las Vegas case agent. The Las Vegas case agent advised me that there was a child kidnapping out of the Las Vegas AO and requested immediate coverage of five leads and any other investigation warranted in this kidnapping. The case agent explained that the victim was Sharon*, a 21-month-old female. The mother of the victim advised the Las Vegas office that the subject, Lynn Jones*, a white female, was a prostitute working in the Las Vegas area. The mother of the victim also explained that, on occasion, she worked as a prostitute and had worked with Jones. Jones had been babysitting Sharon and had babysat Sharon on other occasions in the past as well. But the day that Jones was supposed to return Sharon to the mother, the mother didn't hear from Jones and began to panic. The mother learned that Sharon, along with Jones and Jones' pimp, Frank Cleveland*, a black male, had traveled to California and were staying at a motel in the Los Angeles area. After the mother provided the Las Vegas office with information on Cleveland, the Las Vegas office sent a lead to the Los Angeles office to investigate at the Los Angeles motel. This lead included confirming that Jones, Cleveland and Sharon had in fact checked into this motel and obtaining telephone records of calls made from Jones' and Cleveland's room. Los Angeles agents obtained these records only to discover that five of the telephone numbers called from Jones' and Cleveland's room, were in the Memphis AO. The Las Vegas case agent provided these telephone numbers to me and requested a search to determine the names and any relevant information of the persons registered to these numbers.

Jones' parents were interviewed, and the agents learned that Jones grew up in a fairly wealthy home. Jones' parents had recently bought their daughter a new sports car. The Las Vegas case agent provided photographs of Jones, Cleveland and the victim, Sharon. Jones looked like "the girl next-door " in these photographs. The Las Vegas case agent advised that Las Vegas had no other information tying Jones, Cleveland and Sharon to the Memphis telephone numbers, nor any other connection to the Memphis AO. After writing some notes, which included identifying information on the subjects and victim, I began to cover these leads. I contacted a Memphis support employee and provided the telephone numbers to obtain subscriber information. A few hours later, I received information on two of the five Memphis telephone numbers as the support employee continued to conduct research. A lead of this importance would require contact and an in-person interview at the subscriber's business or residence.

Covering these types of leads required two agents for several reasons, including safety. You never know who you might be interviewing and what possible connection, if any, these individuals might have with Jones and Cleveland. I contacted, SA Karl Clairmont* and asked him to assist. I had worked with SA Clairmont in the past he was assigned to a squad that handles kidnappings. When I contacted SA Clairmont at his residence, he immediately assumed I was calling him to invite him over for a swim in my pool, since in the past I often had pool parties.

SA Clairmont didn't hesitate to assist, and we met at the office to review the information I had obtained from the Las Vegas Division. We began working on the subscriber information from the telephone numbers. The first number we tried was a dead end. The second number led us to an address located just south of downtown Memphis. This address was matched to an alleged beauty parlor located in a two-story building. SA Clairmont and I dressed in business casual, which for the FBI was usually slacks, button-down shirt, and a jacket without a tie. The jacket was primarily to cover your weapon. In those days agents didn't wear a badge on their belts. The badge remained in the cutout slot within the credential holder. Several years later, agents were using badge holders that you could place on your belt next to your weapon. After seeing this I realized it was a good idea, even in Texas, in case someone saw a weapon on your side. They would immediately notice the badge and identify you as some type of law enforcement. When I returned to Texas, with a large majority of people carrying weapons, I felt this was important.

SA Clairmont got into my car and we departed the office in the early afternoon and after a short drive we arrived at the business location. SA Clairmont and I realized that we would stand out in this part of town. During those days in Memphis. whites and blacks didn't integrate very well, but I hope that has changed since. When SA Clairmont and I entered this alleged beauty parlor, we walked into what appeared to be some type of diner. The way we were dressed and the fact that both of us were white and all the patrons were black made it impossible to be inconspicuous. Everyone looked up at us and stared. SA Clairmont and I hesitated for a few seconds, looked around the diner, then immediately went to the small counter where you would place a food and drink order. We presented our credentials and I asked to speak to the manager or owner of the business. The individual behind the counter was friendly and advised that he would get the owner. While we waited, I noticed two things. One was not so important, but somehow stayed in my memory. I could see inside the kitchen and observed a large chest freezer in the kitchen. On top of this freezer were several raw whole chickens covered with flies. The second thing I noticed was a payphone located on the wall. I approached the payphone and looked at the printed telephone number associated with the phone and it matched the telephone number the

Las Vegas Division had provided to me. I wrote the number down in my notepad. Several minutes later we noticed a middle-aged, heavyset black woman coming down the stairs. We introduced ourselves and presented our credentials and she told us her name was Evelyn* and that she was the owner. Evelyn requested that we follow her upstairs so we could talk in her office.

As we walked down the hall toward Evelyn's office, we passed by doors to rooms in the dimly lit hallway. I made some assumptions about what those rooms were used for. We entered Evelyn's office and she invited us to sit down. She was very friendly and cordial and after small talk we realized this establishment was some type of brothel and that she handled many of the business aspects. I explained to Evelyn the purpose of our visit and provided her with details I felt were pertinent in this investigation. I explained that there was a kidnapping out of Las Vegas and the subject(s) called the payphone located downstairs. I further explained that the FBI was trying to determine what connection if any these subject(s) had with this business. Evelyn stated that the payphone downstairs was in fact used for illicit business. I showed photographs of Jones, Cleveland and Sharon to Evelyn and explained that the kidnapped victim was approximately 21 months old. After reviewing photographs of Cleveland, Evelyn admitted she knew of him. She told us that he was a local pimp in this area and that he would frequent this business. In a surprise to both SA Clairmont and me, Evelyn further stated that she had observed Jones yesterday afternoon in the street trying to hustle tricks. Evelyn also mentioned that Jones was very attractive and noticed by her patrons. She hadn't seen Sharon and couldn't recall if Cleveland was around at the time. Evelyn expected Jones to return and I provided her with my business card and asked her to contact me if she saw Jones or Cleveland. She agreed and I felt comfortable that she would follow through on that agreement. Evelyn was very cooperative, and I suspected that in the back of her mind, she might have imagined the FBI helping her in the future.

SA Clairmont and I left the business and immediately returned to the office. We contacted the Las Vegas case agent, my SSA and upper management. I contacted the Memphis Division' Special Operation Group (SOG) SSA and explained the situation and the need for immediate surveillance on Evelyn's establishment. The SOG team is a full-time surveillance FBI team made up of agents. There is also a similar group consisting of FBI support employees. Copies of Jones', Cleveland's and Sharon's photographs were provided to the small surveillance team. The response from the Memphis Division was impressive, but in my 31 years with the FBI, I consider this the norm about how the FBI responds to such matters. The Special Agent in Charge (SAC), Assistant Special Agent in Charge (ASAC) and other agents arrived at the office. The SAC and ASAC are the Division's leaders. A few Divisions have more than one SAC, but most Divisions have more than one ASAC. At the time, the Memphis Division had one ASAC.

I briefed the SAC and ASAC on what I had learned, including the interview of Evelyn. While briefing the Memphis management and the Las Vegas case agent, the Memphis SOG team was set up surveilling Evelyn's businesses with an intense desire to spot Jones and or Cleveland. Just before dusk on that Saturday evening I overheard radio traffic from the SOG team that Jones was standing in the street in front of Evelyn's business, trying to flag down passing vehicles. Jones was dressed in jeans and a white tank top. Almost at that same moment I received a telephone call from Evelyn confirming that Jones was in fact in front of her business. Evelyn was not aware of the presence of our SOG team. The SOG team and Evelyn advised that they didn't see Sharon or Cleveland.

I alerted SA Clairmont and we ran to my car. I began driving toward Evelyn's business. By now dusk had become night. I advised the SOG team that we were en route and that I would be in radio contact with the SOG team. Once SA Clairmont and I arrived, we determined that in fact this was Jones, but we didn't see Sharon nor Cleveland.

I felt the pressure of the Las Vegas agent, Las Vegas and Memphis SACs and ASACs listening to our ongoing reports and relying on me to make the right decision. But I was in control and felt confident in my actions and reactions. There was a lot of radio traffic between the Memphis office operations room and SOG. Too many people talking over each other. I asked them to keep the radio traffic to a minimum unless something of high importance occurred. There were a lot of moving parts and I wanted to maintain surveillance on Jones. We could lose her in a flash if Jones got into one of the vehicles she was flagging down. This could increase the risk if we needed to conduct a car stop, not knowing what the driver's reaction might be. I radioed the Memphis office and spoke to the SAC and ASAC and advised that the individual under surveillance was in fact Jones and I requested that SA Claremont and I, with the backing of the SOG team, could arrest Jones. Surprisingly, the SAC and ASAC advised us to stand down, and that the SAC and ASAC would be responding to the area. SA Clairmont and I were not only disappointed but couldn't understand why SAC and ASAC were willing to risk losing Jones.

Approximately 10 minutes later, SA Clairmont, the SOG team and I observed Jones entering the passenger side of an unknown vehicle that traveled south on Main Street. I called the SAC and ASAC on the radio and explained what had just occurred. Since it was dark, I was only able to provide a limited description of the vehicle. I suggested that we should immediately make a "felony car stop" and arrest Jones due to the fact that we had no knowledge of where the car was heading. During this conversation the vehicle pulled into a parking lot a few blocks away. SA Clairmont and I observed Jones' head go down on the driver side of this vehicle. I relayed this information to the responding SAC and ASAC and again, we were told to maintain surveillance until they arrived. They assured me they would be there within moments. Less than 10 minutes later we observed Jones's head lift back up and the vehicle began to move back toward Evelyn's business. Once the vehicle pulled to the curb, Jones left the vehicle and almost simultaneously the SAC and ASAC arrived on scene. They explained that they now could see Jones and that they were proceeding to make the arrest. It's important to note that neither SASs nor ASACs typically go out and actually make the arrest.

As you can imagine, SA Clairmont and I weren't happy with this decision. We were three blocks away and I drove the vehicle through two red lights to get to the scene where we observed the SAC and ASAC chasing Jones on foot down Main Street. As we drew up alongside the foot chase, I pulled the car over and angled it toward the curb, but as I was getting tunnel vision and focusing on getting out of my car and joining the chase, I neglected to place my car in park. The vehicle began slowly rolling forward. Thankfully, the car stopped at the curb. I ran back and placed the car in park and then jumped out in pursuit. With my running background, I knew I wouldn't have a problem catching up.

Jones had finally been stopped; the SAC pushed her against a wall on Main Street and told her that she was under arrest for kidnapping. The SAC then turned to me and asked, "Do you have your handcuffs?"

I said I did, handed him my cuffs and watched with disdain as he placed my cuffs on Jones. What a joke. I recall thinking to myself at the time, "Gee boss after this can I get you a cup of coffee?"

Jones was handcuffed and the SAC and ASAC placed her in the middle of the back seat of the SAC's car. Placing the subject in the middle of the back seat is not normal procedure. The SAC told me to sit in the back seat with Jones, which is normal procedure, but this positioned me right next to Jones. The SAC and ASAC sat in the front seat with the car in park and the engine running. As I sat in the SAC's car, I could hear radio traffic between several agents stating that they were in a foot chase with Cleveland. They later relayed that they had Cleveland in custody and an agent had been injured in the foot chase. We learned that when the agents approached Cleveland to arrest him, he fled and dropped a handgun before he was arrested.

Now the SAC and ASAC turned toward the back seat and began interviewing Jones, but this was not exactly an interview. They were both extremely hostile and threatening towards Jones. They asked her as to the whereabouts of Sharon. She stated that Cleveland and Jones dropped Sharon off at a home not far from downtown Memphis, but since she wasn't familiar with Memphis she didn't know the address. I knew from the information I'd received from the Las Vegas case agent that Jones had no connection to Memphis. It was understandable that she didn't know where this residence was. But should I jump into the conversation and tell the SAC this? And get my head chewed off? Hell no. If I had more time in the FBI than the SAC I would have.

As Jones kept repeating that she didn't know where the home was, the SAC and ASAC became more and more angry and threatening. The SAC and ASAC told Jones that Cleveland was in custody and that he was being interviewed and threatened that if Cleveland provided this information before Jones, she could go to prison for a very long time.

Several minutes later, radio traffic advised that Cleveland had provided an address. It was getting close to midnight and the SAC and ASAC immediately began driving to this address. It wasn't a comfortable ride for me. A short time later we arrived at the house. It was small and sat up on a slope. Soon after, few more cars with agents also began arriving.

The SAC and ASAC told me to remain in the car with Jones. It was not standard practice to leave one agent in the vehicle with an individual who was under arrest, especially someone of the opposite sex. An ideal situation would have been two SAs, including one female. Regardless, there should have been two agents. It was very uncomfortable sitting next to Jones late at night in the vehicle, especially since Jones' halter top strap kept sliding off of her shoulder almost to the point of exposure. As uncomfortable as I was, I kept sliding that strap back up on her shoulder. I then opened the door and stood outside the vehicle to keep watch of Jones. At one point she asked me to release her. I told her that wasn't possible. It seemed like they were inside the residence for a very long time. Approximately 20 minutes later, the SAC and ASAC came out of the home with Sharon in their arms. After entering the vehicle, the five of us traveled to the Memphis FBI office. The SAC and ASAC proceeded to take Sharon to a medical clinic to determine if she had any injuries and determine her well-being.

SA Clairmont and I brought Jones back to the FBI office and began interviewing her. She explained that she had told Cleveland Sharon was her child. Jones knew that pimps usually paid the prostitutes more money if they thought the prostitute had a child. But Jones didn't expect that Cleveland would tell Jones that they needed to immediately depart for Los Angeles. Jones felt that she had no choice but to travel with Cleveland, even with the child.

During the interview, after Jones' purse was searched, she pulled out several colored condoms and handed them to me and stated that where she was going she wouldn't need these. I told Jones to put the condoms back in her purse. Years later, whenever I ran into SA Clairmont, and even after SA Clairmont was transferred to the Houston FBI office, he would joke and ask if I've used those condoms yet. We had several laughs about that conversation.

After the interview, the SAC briefed the management at the Las Vegas FBI office and then informed SA Clairmont and I that we would be traveling to Las Vegas on the next available flight to return Sharon.

A short time later, SA Clairmont and I departed the Memphis FBI office to go home and pack for Las Vegas. After a few hours at home, we met at the Memphis International Airport. The American Airlines flight departed Memphis that Sunday, June 2, at 7:15 AM for the Las Vegas International Airport. At about the time we arrived in the terminal the SAC and ASAC met us in the terminal with Sharon. Evidently news traveled fast – the AA ticket agent had learned of the successful apprehension of the kidnappers and Sharon's recovery. At the departure gate, AA employees began clapping and cheering.

As on all flights, agents check in at the ticket counter and present our FBI credentials and badge and advise the ticket agent that we are traveling armed. After paperwork is completed, we proceed through airport security and then on to the gate. The gate agent is aware of who we are and the fact that we are armed. This information is also passed on to the pilot and the entire flight crew. This is standard Federal Aviation Administration (FAA) and FBI policy.

Several AA employees knew who we were, and the gate agent moved SA Clairmont, Sharon and I to first class. I had been holding Sharon for a long time. She sat on my lap during departure. After a while, I attempted to hand her off to SA Clairmont. I needed a break. While I was in the process of handing her to SA Clairmont, she began to cry loudly. We realized that she was just comfortable with me, so I kept her on my lap. Of course, the flight attendants were circling around us and congratulating us. Even though FAA and FBI policy doesn't allow armed agents to drink alcohol on flights the flight attendants took very good care of us. Once we were in the air, two flight attendants came over and asked if they could hold Sharon for a while. As tired as I was, I definitely needed a break. I didn't have children of my own, so this was a unique and educational experience for me. I definitely appreciate a single parent on board a flight managing one, two or three children. After the flight attendants took Sharon, I was able to leave my seat and walk around the aircraft for a few moments. Sharon was handed back to me and remained on my lap until we reached our destination.

Once at the gate, the aircraft door opened, but no one exited the aircraft. Instead, two men entered wearing suits and identified themselves as Las Vegas FBI agents. They obviously had been waiting at the gate. They told SA Clairmont and I to stay on the aircraft until all other passengers exited. They explained that Sharon's mother, grandmother and numerous members of the news media were waiting at the gate. The two agents told me to hand Sharon to either the mother or grandmother and we would immediately depart for the Las Vegas FBI office.

After the passengers exited the aircraft, we walked down the jetway and, sure enough, the news media was waiting for us. I didn't expect the large number of reporters with cameras, lights and microphones pointed at me and Sharon as I walked into the gate area. Reporters began asking me questions and placing microphones in front of my face, but following FBI policy I said nothing as I handed Sharon to her mother. Numerous photographs were taken and were in the Las Vegas Review-Journal newspaper, but I'm not in any of these photographs. One photograph in the Las Vegas newspaper shows Sharon in her mother's arms immediately after I handed her to her mother. Like all of my cases that made the news, I kept the newspaper clippings and photographs.

SA Clairmont, the Las Vegas agents and I immediately headed out of the gate area through the airport to their waiting vehicle. We then departed for the Las Vegas FBI office where we briefed the Las Vegas case agent and management of the Las Vegas Division. Both SA Clairmont and I were very tired after a long and stressful 36-plus hours with very little sleep.

It was a long time afterward that I realized how important my investigation was to apprehending the subjects and rescuing Sharon. SA Clairmont and I had conducted a very good investigation. As I was told in the initial contact with the case agent in Las Vegas, the Las Vegas office had set out numerous leads all over the country, but they didn't honestly believe the leads sent to the Memphis Division would be the most important leads in the investigation. The Las Vegas office didn't anticipate that the victim and subjects were in the Memphis Divisions' AO.

Jones was hit with a lengthy sentence, which surprised both SA Clairmont and me. Years later, when SA Clairmont and I discussed this case, we asked each other "Have you received that award money yet." Our answers have always been no.

At the time, SA Clairmont and I had only been agents for three years, so we didn't think much of it. But, as we both realized later in our careers, we should have received more recognition and been awarded by the Las Vegas office. Oh well, just another case in my long and rewarding career.

Approximately nine months later my SSA came to my desk and said he needed to transfer a call to my desk. It was one of the producers of "FBI: The Untold Stories." She interviewed me about filming an episode about this kidnapping. I discussed the work I did and the role the Memphis FBI office played. She told me she would get back to me and when she did, she explained that they were hesitant to pursue the show idea further because of the involvement of prostitutes and the pimp. When I hung up the phone I thought, *Isn't this what they want in these types of true crime shows?*

8

◦•◦

THE TREE AND THE BUSH

In March of 1994, an executive's wife, Sally Marshall* of Memphis, received an extortion letter stating that Marshall and her 18-month-old daughter would be murdered if the family didn't drop off a package with $250,000 at a rural location on the Tennessee-Mississippi border. A map was provided with the extortion letter. A package was created with fake money and dropped at the specific location. No one showed up to retrieve the package. Two months later, Marshall received another extortion letter stating that if Marshall's family didn't leave $250,000 at the same location, Marshall would be raped and her daughter would be kidnapped and sold. The subject(s) again provided a map and wanted the money placed in a black garbage bag.

These two extortion letters were poorly written and very graphic as to what the subject(s) would do to Marshall and her daughter. I was called out and met with the rest of our SWAT team members. We began preparing a plan to conduct surveillance on the area and apprehend any subject(s) that showed up to retrieve the package. The package was a medium-sized black garbage bag. This was the same rural location as before. The drop spot was in a large field enclosed by barbed wire. Even though the subject(s) were not in possession of a victim, the threat was real, so it was important to apprehend the subject(s).

The drop off time was around dusk, and we expected the garbage bag could be retrieved well into nightfall. An agent on the SWAT team, SA Johnny Martin*, and I were chosen to be secreted in this field that featured only a small number of bushes and very few trees. SA Martin and I were the fastest long-distance runners in the Memphis Division. He was a great friend and running partner. We ran almost daily during our FBI-allotted workout time and competed twice a year in the mile-and-a-half run for the FBI fitness test. During my time in the Memphis Division, my fastest time was 8:01, but I hoped I could break the 8-minute mark, which I never did in Memphis. We mostly ran in Memphis neighborhoods near the FBI office and from time to time we were chased by dogs. When this happened, SA Martin would always say, "All I need is to be faster than you." I'm happy to say that a dog never caught either of us.

SA Martin was formerly in the Army and a good and squared away guy. He had made us two ghillie suits to wear during this assignment. This was new to me. Other SWAT team members were set up in a law enforcement helicopter nearby, ready to respond. There were also other SWAT team members waiting in a SWAT SUV located a short distance away.

SA Martin and I donned our ghillie suits and were dropped off well before dusk over a mile from the drop site. We were trying to avoid any counter-surveillance the subject (s) might have set up. We walked and then crawled more than half the distance to set up on the spot where the garbage bag would be dropped. By the time we arrived, it was dusk and we were positioned approximately 15 yards from a barbed wire fence, which was parallel to a rural road on the other side. Our backs pointed to the barbed wire fence.

As we waited, we saw an agent drop the garbage bag. It was in front of us and to our left, approximately 20 to 25 yards from our position. We were confident that our ghillie suits blended in well with the environment as long as we remained still and crouched down in the dark, even though there was some light coming from the moon. There were only scattered bushes and trees in the distance. We were armed with only our handguns and knives. We didn't bring our long weapons, which would have been the MP5. We had two FBI handheld radios and one Night Vision Binoculars. Night Vision Binoculars were a luxury for an FBI SWAT team in 1994. I spent a total of 18 years on two FBI SWAT teams and each year the gear provided to our team got better and better. By the time I stepped off the team, we had some very nice equipment.

We assumed that the subject(s) would approach by vehicle from the road behind us. We also assumed the subject(s) would climb the barbed wire fence, grab the black garbage bag and cross back over the fence and run to their vehicle. Still, you had to prepare for situations not going as planned. That's when we would need to rely on all our training. To ensure that we had reason to arrest the correct subject(s), we had to wait until the subject(s) actually picked up the black garbage bag and proceeded to exit the area before executing the arrest(s). We kept our radio traffic to a minimum and whispered into our handheld radios. We took turns using the one Night Vision Binoculars and most of the time we knelt or crouched unless we wanted to surveil a greater distance. Then we would stand for a very short time and scan the field. We had been waiting for several hours and it was getting late.

We were beginning to think this would be another false alarm. While waiting and kneeling, I handed the Night Vision Binoculars to SA Martin and I crouched down. After a few minutes, SA Martin stood up and began scanning the field, beginning far right of our position. As I looked away from the black garbage bag for what I thought was seconds, my eyes caught movement approaching the bag. A white male was moving slowly towards the bag, and he was now within five yards. I didn't know where he came from. I hadn't heard anyone moving across the barbed wire fence. It was as if he appeared out of nowhere. Since SA Martin was on my left, this blocked the left side of my viewing area. I could tell that SA Martin hadn't seen the subject walking toward the bag. Since SA Martin was still standing, I was worried that the subject would see him or at least see his movements. I began tugging and pulling down on SA Martin's ghillie suit hoping this would signal him to crouch. We had so many layers of clothing, gear and of course the ghillie suit, SA Martin couldn't feel the tugging. Instead, as SA Martin began scanning back toward the black garbage bag he stopped and crouched down. At that point, I knew he had spotted the subject. The subject scanned the area and looked right through us. The ghillie suites worked.

We whispered into the radio to the other SWAT team members waiting in the SWAT SUV and helicopter. We advised them that one white male was approaching the bag. The subject picked up and partially opened the black garbage bag. As soon as he opened the bag, we radioed to the SWAT team members that we were executing the arrest. We began running towards the subject announcing, "FBI stop! Put your hands up!" But he began running with the black garbage bag in hand. We pursued as he ran into the open field instead of back toward the road. This was the same field we had crawled through. Burdened as we were by the ghillie suits and other gear, we weren't catching up with him. We chased the subject for about 30 or 40 yards. We already had our weapons out and I yelled, "Stop or we will shoot." This wasn't true since he had not displayed a weapon. But it worked. He stopped, dropped the bag and put his hands up. Several seconds later the helicopter was hovering above us with the spotlight shining down on us in the middle of the open field. We cuffed him without a fight. It was a successful and exciting arrest. I know it would have been a very bad day if the subject had evaded us.

We later heard that when the subject made an appearance before the Memphis Federal Judge the Judge told our courtroom team that he would have liked to have met the "tree" and the "bush" (SA Martin and me). After pleading guilty, the subject received a sentence of 110 months in a federal prison for extortion.

9

⊸•⊷

SEARCH WARRANTS ON BARBADOS

One July day in 1996, I was sitting at my desk talking on the phone when I heard my SSA say from behind me, "SA Kamel has a passport." Then he walked back to his office. After I ended my call, I walked to his office and asked, "What is this about me having a passport"? He looked up from his desk. "Do you want to go to Barbados for work?" he asked. Now who would say no? Before he could explain I said I was in.

An agent on the white-collar crime squad was assigned to a large international telemarketer fraud case. Victims were located all over the world. The company and owners were first located in Canada, but then moved their operations to the island of Barbados. I had been to Barbados twice on two different cruises and I knew how beautiful the island was, so naturally I was game. I mean, someone had to go. So the case agent, three other agents and I would travel to Barbados.

The company, Worldwide Lottery* (WL), mailed out several million fliers soliciting people all over the world to buy lottery tickets. Often, the mailer stated that they were already winners. WL used every type of ploy to induce their potential victims to purchase these lottery tickets. Victims could pay by credit card or check. Of course, this was highly illegal.

Our group of agents would be working with the Barbadian Police Department (BPD) conducting search warrants at various locations on the Island, including one of the subject's residences. It was unusual for the FBI to be conducting search warrants in a foreign country. Since I was just a grunt in this operation, I didn't know the particulars that

53

enabled the FBI to assist in these warrants. No matter, it would be better to conduct search warrants in Barbados than in Memphis. Naturally we weren't allowed to carry a weapon on the flight into Barbados, but we had our FBI credentials. It was much easier to conduct an operation like this years ago, compared to my later days in the FBI. The plan was to execute the search warrants, seize the computers and documents, house the evidence in an aircraft hangar and, with the help of the United States Customs, fly the evidence back to Memphis. Some or all of us would maintain the chain of custody and travel back to the United States on a United States Customs cargo aircraft. That was the plan. A lot of moving parts. Also, we planned to be there less than a week.

We loaded up and headed for Bridgetown, Barbados. We checked into our hotel and went exploring. The next day we rented vehicles and were assigned to work with at least one Barbadian Police Officer. For me, the not so fun part began when I was assigned a vehicle to go and pick up my partner. Now I have never driven in Barbados, but I have driven many times in the United States Virgin Islands, where you drive on the left side of the road. This takes getting used to, especially when you have been driving 25 or 30 years on the right side on the road. But in Barbados, what made it more challenging was the steering wheel is on the right side of the vehicle not the left side. I cautiously drove and picked up my partner. He was wearing a nondescript police uniform. We introduced ourselves and I began driving to our first destination.

After a short drive we found ourselves in a rural area. I pulled over to the side of the road and just stared ahead at the first roundabout I had ever encountered while driving. Not only was it my first roundabout, but here I was driving on the left side of the road with the steering wheel on the right. A lot of input for me to take in to avoid causing an accident. I had seen many roundabouts in Europe, but I had never driven through any. My Barbadian police officer partner asked, "Why did you stop"? I told him I had never driven through a roundabout and that I was watching what other cars are doing. He started to explain in his thick accent how to negotiate the roundabout, but it was still a little confusing. He kept encouraging me. I turned to him, and asked in a nice manner, "Why am I driving and not you?" To my surprise he told me that he didn't have a driver's license. "How are you a police officer if you don't have a driver's license?" I asked. He told me that it wasn't required as long as his partner had a driver's license. This was just as strange to me as the London Bobbie who accompanied me on my interview in London, and who didn't carry a gun (I'll share more about that in a later chapter). I pulled back into traffic and slowly drove through the roundabout, successfully avoiding other vehicles or any mayhem. I think I was more nervous at that point than during the three gunfights I had experienced thus far in my career. Well maybe not quite.

We went to the subject's residence, but no one was home and I guess we weren't allowed to ram the door down. I didn't need to be hauled away to a Barbadian prison. They are not luxurious like the American prisons. The residence was located on a beach and surrounded by several palm trees and other small residences. Not a bad spot to hang out for a month or ten. As we walked to one side, I noticed a small building next door where a number of women were sunbathing. Since I was on official business and trying to locate the subject of the residence next door, I walked over to them, identified myself with my FBI credentials and asked if they knew the individual next door and if they had seen him. They said they hadn't noticed anyone next door, but they had just recently arrived on the Island. By their accent they were clearly from the United Kingdom. By their looks they could have passed for beautiful Texas women. I'm sure they were thinking, *What the heck, here we are on this isolated part of the Barbados sunning and in the next minute an FBI agent walks up to us and asks questions about the residence next door.* As I've noted before, some days you're the bug and some days you're the windshield. What was I at that moment?

My partner and I conducted our searches for the day and met up with the other agents and officers. We stored the evidence in an aircraft hangar, locked it up after midnight, expecting to fly it out on a United States Customers cargo aircraft the next day. But the next day we learned an emergency court order had been filed in the Barbadian Court to hold the evidence in the aircraft hangar until there could be a ruling by the Barbadian Court. The case agent told us to stand down and that we would just have to wait in Barbados. Not good for the case agent, but for us? I guess we could go snorkeling, swimming, even hang out on the beach. How boring, right? And that is just what we did.

Each evening SA Martin, my running partner, SWAT team partner and good friend and I would leave the hotel and head for the restaurants and bars. And each time we walked out of the hotel we were approached by the same Barbadian asking us if we wanted to buy some weed. We just said no and moved on. On the third night as we walked out of the hotel, he approached with the same question, but we didn't acknowledge him until he became persistent. We stopped and SA Martin told him to move on. "We're the "heat," he said. The Barbadian said, "What?" so SA Martin repeated, "We are the heat, we are the police." The man quickly said, "No you are not." SA Martin said, "How do you know?" This Barbadian pointed to his arm and said, "Because you are white. There are no white police here." We shook our heads and walked off. He had a point. The white population in Barbados was about 2 percent.

I guess I did get punished for having a good time snorkeling, swimming and sunbathing, because we were in the water about chest high and a Man o' War stung me on the back of my neck. It felt like someone had pressed a torch to my neck. I went back to the beach and put sand on it, but for a while I was miserable.

After it appeared the court wasn't going to make a decision any time soon, we packed up and flew back to Memphis. We ended up staying eight days in Barbados and the case agent was able to bring back some of the evidence. I never knew what happened to the rest of the evidence held in that aircraft hangar. Still, not a bad vacation, I mean assignment.

10

1996 OLYMPICS AND MY AUTOGRAPH

On July 19, 1996, one day after I returned from the assignment in Barbados, I left for Cleveland, Tennessee with the Memphis SWAT team for a ten-day assignment at the Ocoee River for the 1996 Summer Olympics. We joined several other FBI SWAT teams located in and around Georgia, which were called up to be part of the 1996 Olympics. The Memphis, Knoxville and other FBI SWAT teams were assigned to the Slalom event to be held on the Ocoee River near Ducktown, Tennessee and approximately 20 minutes from the Georgia border beginning on July 27. The Ocoee is known for whitewater rafting with a beautiful setting in the Cherokee National Forest. We arrived several days prior to the events to train, prepare and study the location. We were housed in a women's college dorm in Cleveland, Tennessee. Since it was summer there wasn't much activity on campus. There was a sign with a list of rules hanging in the lobby of the dorm: No entry on the roof of the dorm, no alcohol and no members of the opposite sex in the rooms. I bear witness that all three of these rules were bent a bit.

We spent little time on campus, but when we had down time, our FBI SWAT team leader and I played a little tennis. Two female college students were also playing on the court next to us. Foolishly, we challenged them to a doubles match. We were confident this would be easy work. What a big mistake. We were beaten down game after game until I finally said, "Okay, let's mix these teams up." We did and had much better matches.

Back on the job, we read intel, filled out the various forms for our security badges and had briefings with the other FBI SWAT teams and local law enforcement. We were there to react to anything or anyone that was there to disrupt the Olympic events, venue, participants, staff or the spectators. We worked with local law enforcement, but the FBI SWAT teams worked mainly with each other. We were more or less an "unadvertised" group.

After we arrived, we conducted training for various situations that might occur. We trained for bus assaults, combat shooting scenarios and transitional shooting with our handguns and MP5s.

We had a command post in the woods with an RV and a few four-wheelers. We were surrounded by beautiful scenery and during breaks we played horseshoes and rode four-wheelers up the hills and through the woods. The Knoxville SWAT team was the lead office at this venue. They came up with comical uniforms for all the SWAT members to wear, so that we could quickly identify other FBI SWAT teams and the civilian population wouldn't know who we were. This was clever, but also a bit silly. We wore our Royal Robbins khaki cargo shorts. Standard gear for the SWAT teams, optional fanny packs (popular back in the day), and backpacks with our collapsible fully automatic MP5s. The highlight, however, were the funny T-shirts they furnished the team as part of the uniform. I still have my T-shirt, which is in great condition. On the back of the T-shirt is a cow standing on a raft and it says "Ducktown Drifters." It was unique and goofy, but it worked, or I thought it worked until one day during the Olympic Slalom competition.

A teammate and I walked the Ocoee River while one of the Slalom events took place. We maneuvered between the river and the large stands and surveyed the fans cheering for their favorite athletes and countries. The distance between the stands and the Ocoee in some areas was as narrow as 25 yards. As I walked with my partner, I heard someone yell out to us. We both turned and there was a girl approximately 12 years old with her mother, standing about two rows up motioning for me to come over to the stands. We looked around, and there didn't seem to be anything of concern going on, but the girl kept motioning for me to come over. As I approached the stands, the girl asked me for my autograph while she held out a pen and a paper note pad. I smiled and said, "I'm sorry, but we're not athletes." She said, "I know y'all are FBI agents and I would like to have your autograph." So much for the stealthy Ducktown Drifters T-shirts. I turned back toward my partner and we both laughed and he said,

"Give her your autograph." I walked up to the stands as low profile as I could be and signed my autograph, hoping no one else had heard what transpired. It was my first and only autograph. I should have just handed the young girl an FBI agent application.

I was amazed at how the Olympians were able to advance through the rapids of the Ocoee River. It took a lot of upper body strength, coordination and determination. As the competition continued, we walked along the river and were approached by an attractive female. She asked if we were part of the American team and we both said, "Yes, we are a two-man Slalom team." She asked when we were scheduled to compete and we told her we had already had our run and did poorly. She was wearing a security pass and we asked her why she was allowed to be in this area. She said she would be presenting the medals at the ceremony. She also mentioned that she was recently in the Miss Georgia Beauty Pageant. We didn't doubt that. She spoke about her life in Georgia, and we continued talking about our run down the river and our disappointing finish. About that time, a law enforcement officer walked up to us and asked if we had any FBI hats we could give him. We said no and he walked off and all three of us began laughing as she now knew who we really were. She asked if I would take pictures of her with her camera when she presented the athletes with their medals. I explained if I was near the stage I would, which I was able to do. Hey, I was just trying to represent the FBI in a good light to a citizen of Georgia.

The Slalom event was thankfully uneventful compared to the main Olympic events in Atlanta. This experience left me with lasting memories.

In 2004, as a member of the Dallas SWAT team, I played a similar role at the Super Bowl in Houston. We spent a week in Houston training on aircraft, trains and buses. These are some of the most difficult settings for arrests and hostage situations. All three have that funnel shape with tight aisles. If we had to quickly enter an aircraft, train or bus with numerous passengers on board to eliminate a threat, there is always a good chance of injury or worse, to both passengers and subjects. I look back at both events and realize how important our roles were to the safety of the attendees and the athletes.

11

FROM PENNIES TO MILLIONS

The year was 1997. I was in the Memphis FBI office when I was assigned to a wire fraud and potential conspiracy case that was also connected to alleged public corruption. I was a co-case agent with a Kansas City SA, Anthony Jensen*. Working almost 26 years as a white-collar crime agent, this was one of the cleverest cases I had worked. It was a complex scheme for 1997, where the computer programming technology didn't come close to matching today's technology.

Our office received a complaint that a local jail was allegedly being scammed out of large sums of money by America Communication Systems (ACS)* in Kansas City, Missouri. The Memphis jail estimated they were being scammed out of approximately $100,000 per month in commissions. ACS had been contracted to provide a pay phone telephone billing system at the jail, which was used by inmates to make local and long distance collect calls. The President of the company was Tony Crawford*. When I began my initial investigation, I learned that the Kansas City FBI office had an open case on ACS, Crawford and other associates. So SA Jensen and I agreed to jointly work this case.

ACS contracted their billing systems to numerous jails, schools, airports and other public facilities throughout the country. For example, an inmate at a jail could pick up a jail payphone and make either a local or long distance collect call. Once the recipient accepted the call, the recipient received a charge on their telephone bill based on the duration of the call. The ACS contracted facilities produced up to 10,000 calls per day. ACS produced the billing records and submitted these records to a third-party company, Dial for America

(DFA)*. DFA billed the recipient of the telephone calls and paid ACS a commission that ranged from 60 to 70 percent of the total billing. ACS in turn paid the jail facility a commission. After an extensive investigation, we estimated the fraud to be almost $10 million dollars, covering a period between 1993 and 1997. The victims varied from recipients of the telephone calls to the jails, airports and other locations that contracted with ACS. We learned that ACS submitted the call record billing statements to DFA, but instead of paying the jail and other facilities commissions based on the statements submitted to DFA, ACS altered the statements to reflect a lower amount. This allowed ACS to pocket the extra money. ACS had also hired a computer programmer, Byron Sullivan*, who worked closely with Crawford to alter the billing. Sullivan wrote several computer programs connected to the ACS facilities to alter the charges on the victim's telephone bills.

These programs included the following:

- Various number of minutes were added to each of the recipients' actual accepted collect calls.

- The recipient was charged for calls in a month that the recipient didn't actually receive a collect call, even though the recipient had accepted a collect call the prior month.

- The recipient was billed for accepting a long-distance call when in fact the call was local.

- The recipient was billed for accepting calls from a particular jail, but the recipient didn't know anyone at that jail. Instead, the recipient had accepted calls from another jail and were billed for calls from both jails.

- Charges for accepting collect calls were billed to random telephone numbers.

Sullivan, acting under Crawford's direction, purchased a CD called "88 Million Household Numbers," then inserted this CD into the ACS computer for billing and created a program that randomly selected telephone numbers to be billed. The recipient's telephone bill listed a customer service 800 number for either ACS or DFA.

Think about this. In 1997, when you received your telephone bill from your telephone provider, you reviewed your bill and looked at the local call charges and especially the long-distance charges. You'd certainly notice an unfamiliar number listed as a long-distance call charged on your bill. But what if the charge was 60 cents? Would it be worth your time and effort to call Southwestern Bell to complain? Probably not.

So was it worth it to call ACS or DFA customer service to dispute the charge? Like many telemarketing scams of the past or even today, the fraudsters were counting on victims not disputing a charge. If telemarketers called 100 people in an attempt to defraud them and convinced even just 5 out of the 100 to comply, they still made money.

ACS speculated that very few people would dispute the added duplicate calls or notice the disparity in the length of the calls. If the bill showed the duration of the call as 11 minutes and 16 seconds when in fact the duration was 7 minutes and 16 seconds, would victims notice. Do you really remember how long you spoke to this inmate? No. Another way they made money was to include a listing of calls from inmates that never occurred.

Each of these calls might cost the victim an extra 25 cents or even $2 dollars. Not much, really. But when scaled up to millions of random phone numbers? Those pennies add up quickly to millions of dollars. It's important to note that some people did in fact call the customer service number and most, if not all, received a credit.

ACS was being overwhelmed with customer billing disputes. When DFA received these complaints they forwarded the complaint to ACS, since ACS was responsible for these "mistakes". In our investigation, we had no reason to believe DFA knew ACS was operating a scam. ACS told DFA that it was a glitch in the system or offered some other excuse. After a while, DFA began wondering why ACS had not fixed this "glitch." It had gone on for nearly four years, and the total amount of fraud added up to almost $10 million dollars. Not bad for writing some billing programs that scammed pennies and a few dollars at a time.

SA Jensen and I were eager to locate and interview Sullivan. We weren't interested in using a search warrant. As noted earlier, I was never fully on board with using a search warrant, anyway. We were both solid interviewers. We hoped that Sullivan would agree to cooperate and surrender his computer to help himself and advance our case.

Sullivan had an apartment in far North Dallas and we had an address, but no apartment number. I flew to Dallas and met SA Jensen who had flown in from Kansas City. With the help of my source, I learned where and when Sullivan would be eating an early dinner. Not knowing where Sullivan was going after dinner, we set up surveillance at the restaurant to follow Sullivan when he left. This type of surveillance should require at least four vehicles, but we only had one. Dallas had grown a lot and changed since I moved to Memphis in late 1988, which made the surveillance even more difficult. SA Jensen wasn't familiar with Dallas. I drove and we arrived at the restaurant and spotted Sullivan's vehicle. We sat and waited. If we lost Sullivan, we might not have another chance to conduct this type of interview.

At approximately 6:00 PM, Sullivan left the restaurant. We began to follow him but lost him within minutes in the busy Dallas traffic. Even though we didn't know Sullivan's apartment number, we knew we could approach an apartment office manager to obtain his apartment number. Of course, that could be risky: the manager could decide to inform Sullivan. But this was no longer relevant since the office was closed. We drove to the apartment complex and continued around the perimeter while we discussed our options. We didn't want to fly back to our FBI Divisions without at least attempting an interview. Admittedly, we were very close to giving up. For whatever reason, I decided to drive by the perimeter of the apartment complex one more time and jokingly said to SA Jensen, "We'll see Sullivan at the gas station located next to the apartment complex."

We were both shocked to see Sullivan putting gas in his car at that very station. We pulled into the gas station and I let SA Jensen out to walk around so that we could approach Sullivan from both sides. I pulled the vehicle up behind Sullivan's and SA Jensen and I walked up to him with our FBI credentials out and identified ourselves as FBI agents. We told him we wanted to speak with him. Without hesitation, Sullivan said, "I knew this day would come." This was a good sign that he would be willing to cooperate. We explained why we were there and he said that he would cooperate and invited us to follow him to his apartment. We followed and entered his apartment and had a successful interview. He pointed out his laptop in the apartment and told us that this was the computer he used to write the programs. He turned the laptop over to us. We had Sullivan's cooperation, admission and the main piece of evidence.

Now that I'm residing in Dallas, I frequently drive by this gas station and apartment complex and reminisce. Crawford eventually agreed to plead guilty and received a four-year prison sentence. In the early 1980s, Crawford had also been convicted in a Federal Court of false statements and Housing and Urban Development (HUD) fraud.

DALLAS DIVISION

12

⸺◦·◦⸺

SECOND KIDNAPPING

I have had several "immediate" SWAT callouts for bank robberies, hostage situations, fugitive arrests and so on. Immediate, simply stated, means "respond immediately to such and such location." But I only had one immediate callout that required at least an overnight that could stretch into weeks. And of course, I didn't have time to go home and pack.

Thankfully, I kept a "go bag" in the trunk of my bureau car, which contained winter and summer clothes, shoes and a shaven kit with toiletries. This was in addition to my SWAT gear. My trunk was always packed. March 10, 2000 was a typical work day. I was driving near downtown Dallas when I received an immediate callout from our SWAT team leader to respond to an area near Troup, Texas regarding a kidnapping. This information and the rally point were all of the information I had, initially, which is typical on SWAT callouts until you reach the designated rally point for a briefing. Dallas to Troup, Texas is approximately a two-hour drive. We rallied at a rural area on Highway 110, where a command post was being established.

My "go bag" came in handy on this callout, since I turned my bureau vehicle onto Interstate 20 and headed east toward Troup. I was one of the first SWAT team members to arrive at the rally point. I began conducting my usual gear and weapons checks. After the responding members of our SWAT arrived, we had a briefing with the SAC of Dallas and the SWAT team leaders. The victim was 18-year-old Kenny McBride* of Troup, Texas. Kenny's father, Craig McBride,

65

was the owner of a plastics company located in Troup. Craig received an unexpected call from an unknown female stating that Kenny had been kidnapped and was being held until Craig provided $200,000 in cash to the kidnappers. Craig was told not to contact law enforcement or Kenny would be killed. Craig would be contacted again with specifics as to where to drop the $200,000.

When the FBI gets involved in a kidnapping such as this, they provide their personnel and expertise. The FBI is excellent at quickly establishing command posts and becoming operational. I have seen this on many occasions. When there is a ransom demand, the victim's family decides if they want the FBI to attempt to rescue the victim and apprehend the subjects without losing the ransom money. That's exactly what Craig wanted the FBI to do.

We didn't know how many subjects we were dealing with. We prepared based on the limited information we had at hand, which included the ransom money drop location, and the very limited information from the unknown female. A short time later, Craig received the expected telephone call. He told the woman that he had the money and was waiting for instructions. She told Craig to drop the money in a laundry machine located behind an abandoned laundromat on Highway 110 near New Summerfield, Texas. The money was to be dropped late on March 10.

After we learned about the drop location, our team set up surveillance on the laundromat, which was in a rural area surrounded by trees. Since the area was so rural, it was dark except for ambient light, and we weren't familiar with the area. In 2000, we didn't have a Google satellite view of the area. We secreted two SWAT team agents in the woods, behind the laundromat dressed in ghillie suits with their eyes on the case containing the money. I was in the back seat of an unmarked SWAT SUV along with other team members. I was fully geared up, which included my main weapon, the fully automatic MP-5 10mm, my handgun and my bayonet knife. The SUV was out of sight of the laundromat, but I could see it from our vantage point. We were in FBI radio communication with the two agents hidden behind the laundromat. One of these agents, Dylan*, was our main sniper and best shot in the division.

During one SWAT firearms training day at the firing range, I was standing next to Dylan and we were shooting at our individual numbered bullseye targets from the 15-yard line. We both were using our Springfield .45s and I looked at my target and then looked at Dylan's target and I laughed to myself, thinking "My score is equal to Dylan's." Then I was truly deflated when I looked out of the corner of my eye and noticed that he had been shooting one handed.

It was getting close to midnight, and we were now looking at early morning. We kept expecting someone to pull off of Highway 110 at the laundromat, walk to the back and retrieve the money. Once we received communications from the secreted agents that someone had actually retrieved the package, we would close in on both sides to make the arrest(s). We knew any and everything could go wrong. There were too many unknowns. How many subjects were there? Were they armed and if so with what? What was in the woods behind the laundromat? The darkness played an apprehensive role in all of this, but I was confident in my abilities and training and I felt the same about the other members of the SWAT team.

As we sat in the vehicle, I asked the SWAT team leader why we weren't utilizing the few Night Vision Goggles (NVG) we had available to us. Based on the look on his face, he wasn't very appreciative of my suggestion. It was as if I was questioning his tactics. Plus, I had only been a member of the Dallas SWAT team for less than two years. Tactically he was good.

A short time later, we got a radio call from the two agents watching the case. They stated that two men were approaching the ransom money. We were now on alert and waiting to hear the "execute, execute" (effect the arrest) command from the team leader. This all happened in a flash. The two subjects didn't enter from Highway 110, and we didn't see a vehicle pull up near the laundromat.

The team leader announced the execute command and we immediately moved to the location. We exited the SUV, and it was a short chase behind the laundromat into the heavy woods. When I was within five yards of the chase, I saw two SWAT team members make a hard tackle on one of the subjects, who then dropped the case. As he was pinned down, I took off with other members running through the woods after the second subject. We weren't familiar with these woods and especially with the darkness it was difficult to ascertain the surroundings. I could see the silhouettes of other SWAT team members running through the woods, and the dancing light from their MP5-mounted flashlights. I had already pulled out my MP5 and flipped on the under the barrel flashlight. I couldn't see the subject, but I knew that I was running parallel and within 20 yards of one of the other SWAT team members. I heard a splash come from where he was running. He had stumbled into a small pond and was now retreating. I continued running toward the noise of others running blindly through the woods. A slight panic came over me when my MP5's flashlight went dead. No matter the circumstances, prior to each mission, I always replace the batteries in my flashlights including the flashlight on my MP5. But somehow, the light went dead and now I was worried that I might draw friendly fire. We have lost far too many agents to friendly fire. I yelled out a few times to identify myself as I slowed my pace. I was able to restore my MP5 flashlight by hitting it several times with my hand.

A short time later, I heard SWAT team members moving back toward the initial arrest site of the first subject. We had one subject in custody. The second subject had evaded us and now we were concerned for Kenny's safety. We now knew there were at least three subjects, including the female. After a brief discussion, the subject was taken away. Another SWAT team member and I were given the task of protecting the case, which lay in the woods a short distance from the laundromat. It's normal policy to remain with the case to protect it from another possible encounter with the remaining subject(s). The case and location were also part of the crime scene evidence. We remained on the ready with our MP5s and radio. We didn't open or touch the case and had no knowledge about its contents. The weather was turning cooler, and I don't know how long we stayed with the case, but it was well over an hour. I learned through radio traffic that the other members of the SWAT team were moving toward other possible locations in an attempt to locate, rescue Kenny and arrest the remaining subject(s). We were hoping for agents to relieve us, so we could join the other SWAT team members. We wanted to get back into the action.

We were eventually relieved and then returned to the command post to learn that the other SWAT team members had "hit" another location - the wrong location. Our ASAC, utilizing "Exigent Circumstances," had provided a telephone number obtained through a trap and trace for a call that was made from one of the subject's telephone numbers. The telephone company unfortunately provided incorrect subscriber information, which included an incorrect address to a home in the area of Troup. The SWAT team members hit that home hard, even utilizing flashbangs (stun grenades). The flashbang creates a blinding flash of light with a loud explosion to temporarily stun anyone in the vicinity.

Besides the damage to the home, I can imagine this aggressive action by our SWAT team in the middle of the night terrified these innocent people. I'm glad I missed that unfortunate incident.

I don't recall if I had any sleep, but we were given new information about Kenny's possible whereabouts. We were told that he had been held at an abandoned house in a rural wooded area outside of New Summerfield. With this information, we all loaded up. We were followed by our Evidence Response Team (ERT) and other FBI personnel and the local sheriff's department.

Only our SWAT team entered the area and began moving toward the abandoned house. We didn't notice any movement nor sound. We surrounded the house with our weapons at ready and closed in. The house was small and truly abandoned. Part of the roof was missing, walls were partially standing, and a portion of the floor was weeds and dirt. We found no one, but there was evidence of fresh food wrappers. I couldn't see any other homes, cabins or structures nearby. The area around the home was partially surrounded by trees, other foliage and small ravines. The SWAT team leader told us to spread out and begin searching in an expanding circular walk.

After what seemed like only 10 or 15 minutes, to my right side, I came across a slightly declining hill. Something caught my eye approximately 20 yards away. Evidently my mind was not processing correctly; it was as if I had blocked out why I was walking through these woods. It didn't make sense what my eyes were fixed on. But, my first thought was, "Why would someone dump a mannequin out here in the middle of the woods?" What at first appeared to be a mannequin was lying face down and one leg was folded backwards. I began walking towards the object and as my mind was processing, I realized that this wasn't a mannequin, but in fact this was Kenny.

As I stood over the body, I could tell he was dead, and it didn't appear to be very recent. I immediately radioed the SWAT team leader with my location and advised that I had found the body. Less than five minutes later the team leader and other SWAT team members descended to where I was standing over Kenny. The SWAT team leader radioed for the ERT and minutes later they arrived and began their work. I was saddened and I know the other SWAT team members were the same. I walked away and headed for our vehicles. We learned that two other subjects had been arrested and that one, the female, was still on the run.

Later that day, the SWAT team leader told members of the SWAT team that the SAC wanted to meet with us. We felt that we had failed to prevent what had just happened. We waited in a room near the command post for the SAC. As we waited, I stared off into space. The room was so quiet you could hear a pin drop. We all had our heads down and felt compassion for the family and seethed with anger toward the subjects. The SAC came into the room and tried to give us some type of pep talk, saying how proud he was of our work. He said, "If this helps in any way, even though the SWAT team didn't apprehend the second subject in the woods, that isn't what led to Kenny's death." The SAC further explained that the investigation and interviews of the subjects determined that Kenny had been killed prior to the money drop. The subjects had intended to kill Kenny from the very beginning. It was still difficult to feel like we had done our best job, but I eventually geared down, packed up my vehicle and headed back to Dallas for that long two-hour drive with a lot on my mind.

Weeks, months and years later, I learned that the subjects received 30-year, 50-year and life sentences. All three were illegal aliens. One of the subjects worked at the plastics factory and knew Kenny. At the end of Kenny's shift that night, some of the subjects had waited outside for Kenny. They approached him and invited him to go out and party. Kenny accepted, not knowing what deadly intentions they had in store for him. Prior to making the first ransom call to Craig, the group killed Kenny by pressing a pipe against his neck and crushing his throat. What a terrible and slow way to die. The female was profiled on "America's Most Wanted" and was captured in Mexico in 2004. She received a life sentence for her role in this murder.

13

DIAMOND SCHOOL, YELLOWKNIFE

Training for my potential undercover roles included attending a Diamond school in Yellowknife, NWT, Canada and a few months later, one in Antwerp, Belgium. I was selected along with two other agents to attend the first course in early September 2002. I was chosen to enhance the roles I would play in undercover work. The course was sponsored by Canadian law enforcement, which covered the basics of diamonds, physical characteristics, the four Cs, grading, sorting, values, and law enforcement issues. It even included a trip to the diamond mine. There were 10 who attended this week-long course. The other seven attendees were various Canadian law enforcement officers.

This was my first and only trip to Canada, and I can't imagine that there are many people who have ventured up to Yellowknife, and definitely not to the diamond mine where I spent a day. Yellowknife sits on Great Slave Lake, the deepest lake in North America and the 10th largest lake in the world. Yellowknife was and still is by far the second most remote place I have ever traveled to. The most remote location was the Ekati Diamond Mine (EDM). I spent a full day at EDM, which is almost 200 miles Northeast of Yellowknife and 125 miles South of the Arctic Circle. It's worth looking up both locations on a map. Good luck finding the EDM. A hint, it's located near Lac de Gras Lake. One road leads into Yellowknife from the Southwest and the only way out of Yellowknife is back on the same road. Growing up in the fourth largest Metroplex in the United States and living in a medium size city, Memphis, I was way out of my element.

Prior to my arrival in Yellowknife, I called the hotel where I had my reservation and asked about the particulars and the weather. The desk clerk told me that the weather is nice in early September and the only problem during that time of year is the "Black Flies." Black flies, not Black Bears? I didn't inquire any further, thanked her and told her I would see her soon. I thought "We have black flies, so what?" Unfortunately, I learned later about this insanity.

I arrived in Yellowknife late in the evening. My hotel was a high-rise that once was an apartment building. The room was nice and spacious with a large den, kitchen, two bedrooms and two bathrooms. I had brought my running clothes, so early the next morning I ran in the area around my hotel to explore.

The week-long classes would include hands-on work with diamonds, including the four Cs (carat, color, clarity, cut), the diamond industry, many investigative aspects of crimes involving diamonds, problems with policing the industry and current issues which included the Kimberley Process. We also had a day-long trip to the EDM.

After meeting the other class members, we all hit it off immediately and worked well together. Maybe since we were part of the law enforcement brotherhood. At the end of the first day, I asked around if anyone else was a runner and no one seemed interested, but the instructor told me about a Canadian law enforcement officer (LEO) who runs daily from the police station. He provided me with his contact number and I met him at the station that evening. When I walked through the parking lot at the police station I noticed several posts with electrical plugs. I asked someone about this and I'm sure they immediately knew I wasn't from around these parts. They told me those plugs were used to plug vehicles in to keep the engine warm during the winter. Welcome to a place that gets down to -40 degrees in the winter. Who can live in this weather? I guess on the other hand people will ask who can live in Dallas when the weather gets over 100 degrees, 30 or so days during the summer. They had a small dressing room where I changed, and we took off for a run.

The narrow running path circled a scenic lake with trees in the background. We ran close to the lake and had to jump or step up on rocks to cross to the other side and continue running. This was a nice extra workout. We talked about our jobs, Yellowknife and many other subjects. It is always nice to have a running partner where you can chat it up. During the entire run we were in deep conversation and as another runner passed by in the opposite direction, I heard the runner say "clear." The LEO responded with "clear" and we continued running and talking. Another mile or so later, two runners passed in the opposite direction and said "clear" and again the officer replied in a like manner. Another mile or so later, the same thing happened and I finally asked him what "clear" meant. He said it's customary when runners pass by you to say "clear" if you haven't seen any bears. Bears? Another awakening. I'm used to being chased by a dog every now and then and I have ended up on the hoods of three cars while running over the years, but bears?

Now my head was on a swivel. I asked what we should do if approached by a bear. He said the best approach is to make yourself as big as possible by raising your arms, standing tall and walking backwards. Note taken, but I'm barely 5'9". I ran with him for a few more days and happily never saw a bear.

The next day we were to fly to the EDM, which began operations in 1998. The only way to reach EDM is by air. In the winter, supplies are brought in by the ice truckers. We met at an aircraft hangar next to the Yellowknife airport. Our small twin-prop plane was there, but the pilot told us to stand down since the weather to the mine was under thick clouds, and if it didn't clear soon we would have to cancel the trip. We were all pretty bummed, so we hung out in the hangar. But after about an hour the pilot told us it was clear enough to leave for the mine. He explained, though that if he entered clouds near the mine it would be difficult to land and we would have to turn back.

We boarded the plane and as we flew we were in and out of the clouds. All you could see was the flat tundra with hundreds of very small pockets of water. It was like the opposite of a desert with a flat, rocky surface and pockets of water everywhere. The area between Yellowknife and EDM were completely void of civilization. As I looked out the aircraft's window I thought if we went down out here we'd be in a world of hurt. Finally, I could tell we were descending, but the cloud cover was thick, so I was wondering if the pilot was going to turn back. It wasn't until the last second that I could see the ground just underneath us and then we landed. The pilot knew what he was doing. As we departed from the aircraft all I could see was the EDM facility. But apart from that, there were absolutely no distinguishing landmarks. Before we walked towards the facility the pilot gathered us together and warned us not to leave the facility grounds and start roaming around. "You will become confused and lost even a short distance away, since there are no landmarks," he said. Another note taken.

We entered the impressive EDM facility and were given a tour of the operations, history, security and employment. There are over 250 employees at EDM at any given time. We were told that employees come to the mine to work for one-to-three-month shifts, since there is housing and a cafeteria at the facility. It looked like a nice setup for the employees, but not for me. No thanks. We had a good lunch in the cafeteria. We saw piles of rough diamonds sitting on a table in a room behind glass. I couldn't even imagine the value of all those rough diamonds. We were shown a glass case surrounding a piece of petrified wood. We were told that this piece of wood was found in the early stages of digging in the mine and dated back 50 million years. I couldn't believe what I was looking at.

After lunch we met with security for a briefing before we entered the building housing the primary rock crusher, which had a conveyor belt that ran next to a narrow walkway. This rock crusher breaks the large rocks into manageable pieces that are sifted through to remove and sort the rough diamonds. They provided us with our security pass to be worn around our neck, reflective vests and hardhats. We would be walking on the narrow path next to the rock crushers. We were instructed to walk in single file since the rock crusher would be operating and some of the debris lands on the walking path. We were further instructed not to stop and bend over to tie a shoe or for any other reason. If you needed to do this, we were to call out to security so that they could stand next to us. They didn't want you to reach down and pick up any debris, which could easily contain rough diamonds. Naturally it was very loud in the rock crusher facility and the rock crusher and conveyor were operating much closer to the walking path than I expected. With EDM producing 10,000 carats of diamond per day, I couldn't imagine how many carats of diamonds were in the debris we walked on. As we exited the rock crusher faculty, they told us to stop and pull our shoes off. Security came up and closely inspected the bottom of our shoes to make sure there were no small rocks or pebbles caught in our shoes' tread. The value of our shoes could have increased dramatically.

After leaving the rock crusher facility, they took us to the large mine which has a diameter of more than half a mile and a depth over 1500 feet. What a great view. When I looked down to the bottom of the mine, I could see trucks at the bottom that looked like ants. I stood next to one of these trucks at the facility, which is 12 feet tall.

Later in the day we flew back to Yellowknife with slightly better skies. The next day we were back in the classroom and that evening one of the students in the class invited everyone over to his residence for a party and cookout. I walked into his backyard where the small party was gathered, but I don't remember speaking to anyone because my eyes immediately went up to the night sky. I couldn't believe what I was seeing for the first and probably my last time: the Northern Lights. Pictures do not do the reality justice. The different colors constantly dancing in the sky were indescribably beautiful. One of the Canadian LEOs must have seen me with my neck bent back; he came up to me and said, "I can take you out of the city to an area without the lights of Yellowknife if you like."

So later that night another FBI agent and I jumped in the Canadian LEOs' large SUV. We drove about 10 minutes outside the city and pulled into a lightly wooded area. We exited the SUV and, sure enough, the view was even better. It was so dark outside you could only see maybe 10 feet in front of you. As we stood next to the SUV staring into the sky, I noticed a small lake maybe 25 yards or so from where we were standing, and I started walking to the lake. The LEO asked where I was going. I told him I wanted to walk to the lake. He said "No," and warned me that there are bears in this area. Here we go again with the bears. I said I would hear the bear, but he explained that the bear would be on me before I could hear him. I can see the headlines: "Dumb FBI agent eaten by bear outside of Yellowknife." So instead, the other agent and I hopped up on the hood of the SUV and lay back to look up at the sky. I noticed what I thought were meteors and mentioned it to the LEO. He said, "Those aren't meteors, those are satellites." He went on to explain how you can tell the difference, and sure enough I saw others cutting all the way across the sky. What a bonus, knowing that I'll probably never see this again. We stayed for about half an hour or so, then headed back. What an experience.

I stayed in Yellowknife through the following weekend and that Friday evening a few of us went to a bar and somehow I ended up at a table with eight or ten women. One of these women was chatting me up and asked me to go to a big party tomorrow night. I wasn't interested and declined. I met another woman who spoke broken

English. She had recently arrived from Brazil and was staying with her sister who recently moved to Yellowknife. That seemed strange to me - moving from Brazil to Yellowknife. We agreed to meet for lunch the next day. That morning I was about to go for a run and my phone rang and it was the woman at the bar from last night. She asked me again if I wanted to go to the party. Once again, I declined. Besides, I had plans.

The Brazilian woman picked me up and we went to a small restaurant for lunch. We left the restaurant and began walking down the street, which had little activity, but we saw a few shops along the way and wanted to walk for a little while. As we were walking, the horrible attack from hell came. Flash back to the hotel employee who told me the weather would be great for my arrival in Yellowknife but warned me about the black flies. A huge swarm of very large, very angry black flies were all over us in an instant, like Alfred Hitchcock's movie *The Birds*. Panic was an understatement. Flies were all over her long, black hair. I tried to swat them off her hair, but it seemed like there were thousands. Every man and woman for themselves, or be the southern and noble gentleman and protect the women? This was an easy decision. I was a Texan: protect the women. I grabbed her hand and pulled her close and as she was screaming I said, "Run." But where? I saw a shop about 30 yards away and she held on tight to my hand and we hit that door at full speed. The few people that were in the shop looked up at us and probably thought we were insane, dumb tourists. Forget about bears, this was worse. We stood at the window and stared out until the flying monsters left, probably in search of other fools or tourists.

Later that evening my new friend picked me up and we went to Bullock's Bistro for dinner. I had eaten at Bullock's Bistro a few days prior with some of the members of the class. We were told the hole in the wall restaurant had great food, but jokingly warned to watch out for the two ladies that ran the place. "They can seem rude," we were told, "but that is their personality and it's just a way to have fun with their customers."

The first time I ate at Bullock's Bistro I sat at the bar with another agent and the rest of our group sat at the table behind us. I ordered a whitefish and fries plate with a beer. As I was waiting, I mentioned to the lady behind the bar about my beer order. She said, "I know you ordered a beer, get it yourself," then pointed with her head to the glass refrigerator at the end of the bar. I sheepishly stood up, walked to the refrigerator, pulled a beer out and sat back down. The agent sitting next to me just laughed. By now I was on guard. I watched her as she picked up a plate of food from the grill behind her and handed it to me. I looked at the plate and nervously said, "Excuse me ma'am, this isn't what I ordered." She looked at me and said, "I know what you ordered, take the plate to the table behind you and hand it to them." I stood up again, beaten down, and walked a few steps to the table, which was filled with members of our group, and handed them the plate of food. My food came and it was very good. One of the guys sitting behind us handed his plate to the lady behind the bar and she refilled it with fries. I asked him, "How did you get the extra fries?" He said, "Just ask." Those fries were so good, should I risk a possible storm? I risked it. The lady stared at me, snatched the plate from my hand, filled with more fries, turned and gave me a half wink. These two ladies were a lot of fun. They reminded me of one of my favorite hole-in-the-wall lunch restaurants in New Orleans: Mothers. You kind of feel like family in Bullock's and Mothers.

My Brazilian friend and I sat at the bar and of course I ordered the whitefish plate again. I would love to go back just to eat at Bullock's Bistro. I'm not gonna get this back in Dallas. I enjoyed the training and I actually learned something. Not just how to get extra fries.

14

---◦•◦---

DIAMOND SCHOOL, ANTWERP

The last day of class in Yellowknife, two of the Canadian LEOs asked me if I was going to the International Gemological Institute (IGI) Rough Diamond Course in Antwerp, Belgium in mid-January 2003. I said I don't know anything about the course and I doubt the FBI would sign off on it, but I would love to go. I could further enhance my limited diamond skills for undercover roles. The Canadian LEO instructor told me he could email FBI management recommending me to attend this course. I said that would be great and thanked him.

Sure enough, weeks later the recommendation came in and after a few steps I was approved to attend. Antwerp is the diamond capital of the world; almost 90 percent of the world's diamonds pass through Antwerp at least once. So, a diamond school in Yellowknife in September 2002 and four months later, another diamond school in Antwerp. What a great job I had. I stayed in touch with the two Canadian LEOs who had attended this course. They were flying to Brussels from Canada and arriving on the same day. I was scheduled to fly from Dallas to Brussels and take the train to Antwerp, which was about an hour ride. I would be in Antwerp for the two-week course and a day after I returned to Dallas I would fly to New York City for a week-long work trip. This was going to be a long three-week period. The LEOs were scheduled to arrive in Brussels close to my arrival time, so we agreed to meet in the luggage area and take the train together to Antwerp.

I remembered my flight vividly. The weather was turning bad, with light snow and ice. I boarded the aircraft, which was mostly empty—I was the only one in my three-seat row. We pushed back from the gate and the pilot announced that our aircraft needed de-icing. We waited and waited, and the pilot came back and stated that we were 64th in line for the deicing, so we would be sitting a while. I was thinking, "How often do aircraft at Dallas Fort Worth airport need deicing?" I pictured some guy outside reading the instructions on how to operate the deicing equipment. Even after we were de-iced the pilot came back and told us that we were still in a long line and if we went back to the gate we would lose our place in line. The pilot also announced that the ground crew was bringing out a second de-icing equipment. We waited for almost five hours. That was the longest I had sat on an aircraft waiting to depart. Naturally I missed my connecting flight and arrived in Brussels much later than expected. I waited for my luggage, which never appeared. As I was walking to the office to fill out the missing luggage paperwork, I saw the two LEOs waiting for their luggage. Both of our flights had been delayed and we ended up in the luggage area together. The airlines gave me a package with clothes and miscellaneous items. I told the airline that I would be in Antwerp and that they would need to bring the luggage to my hotel. The luggage showed up about 24 hours later.

The Rough and Polished Diamond Course was held in a building in the center of the Antwerp Diamond District. The class instructor was very knowledgeable in all measures of the diamond industry and well-traveled and worked with many diamond mine facilities. Including myself, there were eight students. We were a diverse group. I was the only American. The others included the two Canadian LEOs, three Belgium, one French and one Democratic Republic of Congo student. The Canadian LEOs and I were the only law enforcement participants. This information wasn't shared with the other students, only the instructor.

During my two weeks in Antwerp, the two LEOs and I met in the diamond district with member(s) of the Diamond High Council, Government Valuators, Belgium Police, toured and met members of the Antwerp offices of BHP Billiton Diamonds, De Beers, Rio Tinto and a rough diamond cutting lab.

With only eight students, I was able to participate more in class discussions and work closely with the rough diamonds presented to me. We covered many topics involving the diamond industry. For example, I learned more about the Kimberley Process (KP). The KP is an international initiative to create transparency in the diamond industry to prevent the trade of "conflict diamonds," better known as blood diamonds. Blood diamonds are diamonds harvested in war zones, such as Sierra Leone, Angola, The Democratic Republic of Congo and Liberia, and used to fund warlords or rebel army's insurgencies. An initiative began around 2000 to prevent the trade of conflict diamonds. The KP was named after these meetings that were held in Kimberley, South Africa. An agreement was signed by more than 80 countries to only trade rough diamonds that have been KP certified, which meant they must be shipped in sealed containers with the KP certification. In summary, the KP certificate states that the rough diamonds are free of conflict or blood diamonds. In 2006, the movie *Blood Diamonds* was released, which gives an excellent account of the blood diamond trade.

One of the highlights of the class was the training I received in how to cut a rough diamond in order to maximize its value using the four Cs. I didn't actually cut rough diamonds, but I was given rough diamonds to study. After studying the rough diamonds, I had to first determine the shape I wanted to cut the diamond into to minimize the waste and maximize the value. You want to cut to create brilliant and reflective facets. After drafting where my cuts would be, the class instructor seemed impressed, but I'll still keep my day job.

After each day of class the three of us walked back to our hotel and I would put my running clothes on and knock on one of their doors, which were just down the hallway from my room. Every evening they were in the room drinking Crown and one of the guys was chain smoking and here I was going for my run. After I finished my run, I would shower, and we would all go to dinner. After dinner we would always end up in a pub.

One evening we were on our way to a pub and traveling by cab. All three of us were sitting in the back seat, and for some reason the cab driver was talking smack about President George W. Bush's policies on Iraq. I had enough of his mouthing and began making some strong comments back to the cab driver. While I was doing this the two LEOs were kicking my feet, trying to get me to shut up. Too late. The cab driver stopped and said, "Get out." Thankfully we didn't have far to walk to the restaurant. But the night went further downhill. After dinner, as usual, we walked to a nearby pub. It was a typical dimly lit pub; small and narrow with the bar located in the back. Early on, there weren't many people in the pub. We sat at the bar and ordered drinks, then started talking to the bartender. He was maybe in his 30s and introduced us to his girlfriend who was standing close by. He told us that they owned the pub. They were a sharp looking couple. We had a nice conversation with them. I know I was getting a little tipsy and I assumed the LEOs were too, since they had been drinking since after class.

After about an hour and a half we paid up and said goodbye to the owner. We planned to just grab a cab back to the hotel. As we walked toward the exit, there were three guys standing in front of it who looked like they weren't in the pub to enjoy drinks. They were big, thug-like characters. As we approached to walk past them, they stopped us and said in broken English that we have to pay to leave. They had a Russian accent. A cover charge to leave the pub? I could tell they weren't joking, but the bigger LEO said, "No, we're not paying to leave." They then blocked the door, which had a narrow entrance. Only way to get outside was through them. I don't recall the amount they wanted. It wasn't extreme, but it was bullshit. One of the guys grabbed the bigger LEO and in my slightly drunken state I went to push hard to get the guy off the LEO. I barely caught him but slid off him and hit the wall. They weren't moving until we paid. I quickly walked back to the bar and told the owner about the situation. He sheepishly apologized and said he couldn't do anything about it. "Those guys are from East Germany," he said, "and they have groups that do this at various pubs." It sounded like the Mafia to me. I went back to the front and pulled the LEOs back and told them what the owner had said. We paid and left. I'm sure the situation could have been worse for us. Naturally, we didn't go back to that pub.

I couldn't believe how many diamond/jewelry stores there were just one street over from the diamond district. On one street all I could see were diamond/jewelry stores lined up on both sides as far as the eye could see. They were small, but nice in appearance. If you want to buy an upscale diamond or diamond-encrusted jewelry, you could do worse than take a vacation to Antwerp and shop at these diamond/jewelry stores. I'm sure the prices would be much lower than in the United States.

Walking around the L shaped diamond district with the two LEOs we were amazed at the well-dressed men walking around with briefcases, many made of aluminum or metal. We assumed there were diamonds in these cases, but they must know what they are doing. The area was just so easy to access knowing what was housed inside these buildings. Three weeks after they returned to Canada and I returned to Dallas, there was a large heist of safe-deposit boxes in the Antwerp Diamond District. Over $100 million worth of loose diamonds were stolen. Gold, silver and jewelry were also stolen; it was the largest heist in history. The LEOs and I discussed the heist and joked that just a few weeks prior, we had talked about how the diamond district looked so vulnerable. We later learned the thieves were apprehended. Turns out they spent 18 months preparing for this heist. They might have walked right past us on a few occasions. When you read about the robbery it is something right out of the movies. I'm surprised a movie hasn't been made about this heist.

About six months after Antwerp, I received sad news about one of the LEOs I hung out with. The LEO (the heavy drinker/smoker) died of a massive heart attack. He was the same officer who had hosted the party in his backyard while I was in Yellowknife.

15

◦•◦

SPACE SHUTTLE COLUMBIA

It was approximately 8:00 AM on Saturday, February 1, 2003. I was lying awake in bed, just about to rise and start the morning in my Plano, Texas home when I heard a rumble and felt the house vibrate. I thought, "That jet flew unusually low over my home." But, since there are frequent commercial and private jets flying overhead, I didn't think much of it. While I was in the kitchen preparing my usual large breakfast and watching the TV, the news reported that the Space Shuttle Columbia had just exploded over the Dallas area toward Eastern Texas. I immediately realized this was the rumble I heard and felt. I watched the news in complete disbelief.

A few days later, calls from management at the FBI Dallas office sought volunteers to respond to East Texas. I volunteered, not knowing what my role would be nor how long I would be in East Texas. The FBI Dallas division established a command post in Hemphill, Texas, a population of approximately 1,200 and about 20 miles from the Louisiana border as the crow flies. Initially, I was told that I would be evaluating and entering information in the FBI database for the space shuttle recovery process. I packed for East Texas, expecting to be gone for a week or longer. As I departed Dallas for the command post, I didn't have a hotel or place to stay. Knowing that support personnel, news media and other law enforcement would be arriving in this area, the chances of finding a hotel would be slim to none. I reported first to the command post where an ASAC was in charge. I knew this ASAC from when I was in Memphis. At one time he was my SSA in Memphis and we had always worked well together.

He welcomed me and asked if I wanted to work in the command post evaluating and entering data in the FBI database, or if I preferred to work outside searching the woods of East Texas for space shuttle debris and the remains of the shuttle crew. As well as he knew me, he knew what my answer was going to be. Without hesitation, I said, "Put me outside with the search teams."

I learned of a motel room available in San Augustine, Texas. Even though San Augustine was 25 miles away I felt lucky to have found an available room. A made a phone call and reserved that motel room. Another agent and I were assigned to oversee a group of approximately 50 Native Americans to conduct grid searches in the thick woods of East Texas. There were several other teams conducting these searches at different grid coordinates. After attending a meeting directed by NASA officials, we were briefed on how NASA wanted the search handled. We were shown a large board with photographs of various parts to the Columbia Space Shuttle. These parts were broken down into categories such as computer components, parts that may contain liquids such as fuels etc., and of course we were briefed on searching for the remains of the seven crew members. This was a well-organized and coordinated search. We were given GPS equipment and yellow caution tape and we had our FBI hand radios. We were instructed to enter the GPS coordinates of the location where space shuttle debris was found, make written notations and arrange the yellow caution tape appropriately until a secondary search team could come back and retrieve the debris. We were also instructed that if we located any debris that might appear to contain fluids used in the space shuttle, we would need not only to enter the GPS coordinates but place a priority on the site and radio the NASA secondary team to immediately recover this debris. If we located computer components, we were told to enter the GPS coordinates, retrieve these parts and bring the parts back to the command post. And of course if we located any human remains, we were to enter the GPS coordinates remain on site and radio the secondary team to immediately respond to our GPS location.

The locals told us to watch out for "mister no shoulders" (snakes). In this part of East Texas we would be on the lookout for Copperhead and Cottonmouth snakes, due to the fact that we were walking through thick brush and disturbing their homes. I ran across two.

There was a large group of Native American volunteers, mostly from Oklahoma, that traveled to Hemphill and other areas of East

Texas by bus. The other agent and I were in charge of a group of approximately 50 Native Americans and all tasks associated with these searches. This group worked together each day covering several grids. If you knew the history between the FBI and Native Americans, then you knew there could be apprehension from both sides. We had heard stories of agents working on reservations and how difficult those assignments could be. We also all knew about the two agents who were killed in 1975 on an Indian Reservation in South Dakota. But we were all open-minded and wanted to work alongside this group who had volunteered for these searches.

On day one, I dressed in my Royal Robbins pants, SWAT t-shirt and a light wool jacket with my SWAT-issued .45 pistol in my tactical holster. I didn't see a need for the MP5. I also carried a large buck knife, water, radio, backpack, GPS tracker, yellow warning tape and other miscellaneous items. I wore my SWAT boots, which were a poor choice I learned on the first day. We were loaded on buses and taken to our starting grid location. When we arrived, I didn't know anything about the group I was assigned to, including their skill set and what training, if any, they'd had. But I could tell immediately they knew what they were doing. They were dressed in yellow jackets. Two leaders from their group lined them up approximately five yards apart and walked forward in each grid search. The other agent and I walked slightly behind the Native Americans. Being in such a wooded and rural area, versus a city, these space shuttle pieces would be easy to identify. They had no business being in this rural area.

When a possible space shuttle piece was found, the whole line signaled to stop and either the other agent or I looked at the item in question. As instructed, I took notes and entered the GPA coordinates. I marked the area with the yellow tape and announced that we were ready to re-assemble the line and move forward. Each day we made frequent stops either after we found debris or to re-line up. I found a few pieces of piping, which were priority pieces according to NASA. I followed procedure so they could collect them asap. I also found a component that looked like a computer board. This thin piece appeared to be one and a half feet by one and a half feet. After I entered the GPS coordinates and wrote some notes, I placed the computer board in my backpack. It was difficult to imagine where this computer board belonged on the space shuttle, what its functions were and how it appeared as if it just floated to the ground. I never really grasped that I was looking at undisturbed space shuttle debris nor that I had held a piece of a computer component from the space shuttle. These pieces were in outer space and now sat undisturbed in the middle of rural East Texas. I was just focused on doing my job and doing it to the best of my ability. Now, however, I can reflect on those days. The photos in this book were taken just as the debris was found.

Once a grid was completed, we moved to the next grid to search. Each time, the line would be disrupted; either from finding debris or moving through an area that was heavy brush. They were so efficient in these grid searches; regrouping and reorganizing as needed before moving forward. We walked the line with very little deviation so that we wouldn't miss anything. No matter how thick the nasty East Texas brush was, we walked through it. Once you get tangled up in the thorn bushes, which I did on too many occasions, it took some work, and a few times help from the group to get out of it. Forget wearing a short sleeve shirt. My wool jacket was like a magnet for the thorn bushes. When we came across trees we stopped and looked up to see if branches caught any of the space shuttle debris. The ground was wet and muddy, and these fields were mostly, if not completely, private property. There were numerous barbed wire fences to traverse. On many occasions, in these isolated fields and brush, I saw complete skeletal bones of cattle and other scattered bones.

After a short time our group became comfortable working together. I really enjoyed working with the Native Americans. They were good at keeping the line together. Walking constantly through mud and crossing various small streams, my boots, socks and feet were soaked, which made it difficult to walk. When I arrived back at the command post to check in and log in the debris we had found, I spoke to the ASAC about the problem with my boots. I already had cuts and blisters on my feet. Those SWAT books sucked in these conditions. The ASAC told me that others had also complained about their footwear. He told me that he would see what he could do about getting a pair of boots that could handle the environment. I gave him my boot size, but I didn't expect the FBI to buy us boots. As I left the command post, a number of us were invited by members of the Hemphill community to a feast they were preparing just outside the command post.

This community grilled and cooked a variety meats and other food and invited us to eat, relax and enjoy. I was honored and impressed to be taken care of by the people in the community. In fact, each evening

I was there, community members took care of us.

It was now nightfall. I was dead tired and needed to head to my motel in San Augustine, but I wasn't familiar with the area. I asked two young women for directions and they offered to lead me all the way to San Augustine. I tried to refuse the generous offer, but they insisted. I have to assume they had never met an FBI agent and perhaps that somewhat excited them. I followed behind them and we arrived at my motel and visited for a while. Then I thanked them as they departed back to Hemphill. This was such a friendly community.

The next morning when I checked in at the command post, I met with the group and we loaded onto the buses and headed out for another day of grid searches. Our team was bonding together. As we came across a larger than usual stream, we found a way to cross the stream using a fallen tree. Back then, my balance and skills were sharp; I was sure I could cross back and forth over this tree without falling into the water. So after the Native Americans crossed single file over the stream, it was now up to the two agents to cross. The Native Americans didn't call us by our names, they just called us Agent. First up was the Houston agent and they were calling out, teasing and putting pressure on him to cross and not fall. We all enjoyed the hooting and hollering. He almost made it across but splashed down just at the other side's edge. That put more pressure on me to cross. I was doing fine until I neared the other side. As I began to fall, I jumped and barely cleared the stream. I still had my pride left.

This reminded me of something I had learned. Several years ago there was a football coach who painted a long, narrow line on the ground and had his players walk on the line without stepping off. Of course, they could walk this line easily without stepping off. But if that line was a beam or log of a similar width, and the beam or log was suspended several feet above a ditch or, say water, suddenly it would be more difficult. Your mind plays tricks on you. You're now putting pressure on yourself when you know you could walk this line just fine if it was lying on the ground versus being suspended in the air. The lesson served me well on this particular day.

After we found more space shuttle debris and I entered in the GPS coordinates, we finished the day and I returned to the command post. When I checked in, I happily found a pair of new Muck boots waiting for me to use for the rest of the search. What a difference those boots made.

The next day's grid search had plenty of thick shrubs, including the dreaded East Texas thorn bushes. I became caught up in thorns one too many times and had to work myself out like others on the team.

While walking through dense, almost chest high shrubs, I was unable to see any of my group in front of me even though they were wearing their yellow jackets. Suddenly, they began yelling at me, "Shoot it, shoot it!" As I sensed their urgency, they continued to shout, "Shoot it!" My mind began to race as I was scanning the waist high shrub. I was trying to comprehend, "Shoot what? Why? What is going on?" Not knowing what the shouting was about, I did what my training told me, I jerked the .45 from my tactical holster. That's when I saw it. But what did I see? I saw the bushes moving rapidly and violently back and forth back and forth and these movements were heading right towards me. With the .45 out, I was fully focused on whatever was heading towards me. Per my training, my finger was off the trigger and no matter what I was about to encounter, I knew I had to be careful of my surroundings if I needed to fire my weapon. I might have to make a "Surgical Shot" to avoid any possible collateral damage.

As the bushes continued dividing all the way up to where I was standing there it emerged: a hairy Feral Hog, which appeared to weigh several hundred pounds. It was snorting as it came within feet of me. The hog then turned and continued to run through the thick brush. I'm glad I remained somewhat calm and didn't fire my weapon.

As the hog ran away the members of the search team were giving me a hard time for not shooting it. I jokingly told them, "If I shot a hog that big, I would have just pissed it off." They then began telling how they could dig a pit and cook the hog in the pit, which didn't interest my palate. Besides not having a legitimate reason for shooting this large hog, I would have been razzed for several years.

After we had our laugh, we lined up and continued the grid searches. From time to time we would hear radio traffic stating that HR (human remains) were found and the coordinates were being sent for the medic teams at the command post. It didn't take long for the large number of news media teams to figure out that HR meant human remains and they would respond and attempt to get as close to the area as law enforcement would allow. A short time later, the radio code HR was changed. During one of my grid searches, I heard a radio transmission of human remains found with coordinates located in a grid bordering my grid. This was one of the space shuttle's pilots and

I was told later that evening that this pilot was mostly intact, but without any clothing. I wondered, how it was possible that a human body could endure such high velocity force and remain mostly intact? I remained in East Texas conducting these grid searches for several days before returning to Dallas. It was yet another unique experience working as an FBI agent. I later received a well written letter and certificate from NASA thanking me for my role in the search.

16

EIGHT MILLION DOLLAR EMBEZZLEMENT

If you have greed, you have a need for money. While assigned to the Frisco RA of the Dallas Division, I encountered greed that was downright cold, harsh and heartless. The victims in this case were average paycheck to paycheck citizens, the wealthy, friends, neighbors and a large bank. When the opportunity presented itself, Gary Myers* was there to steal it and then to spend it. I can't imagine what enters a person's mind to cause such damage to people in your life.

It was the summer of 2011, when I opened this case after I received information that Myers*, the President and Chief Financial Officer (CFO) of Progressive Products* (PP), a publicly traded company, had embezzled funds, which caused a loss of over $8 million. Myers held both titles of President and CFO of PP. PP was based in the Dallas area with the company's Board of Directors located in California. Due to Myers' embezzling, PP was having major financial difficulties even though PP's quarterly reports to Security Exchange Commission (SEC), indicated that PP financials were in the "black" with positive earnings. Myers had signed and certified these falsified monthly reports. This information was also forwarded to the PP Board of Directors and the bank that held PP's revolving line of credit. No one was aware that Myers was stealing PP funds and driving the company toward insolvency and later into bankruptcy. I interviewed numerous victims, witnesses and Myers. I reviewed and assessed numerous bank records and credit card statements. During this time period the bank's line of credit wasn't being paid. The bank lost over $2 million.

In early 2007, PP, through Myers, had a $2 million revolving line of credit, with only the interest being paid until the entire loan was due at its maturity date. Myers was required to report monthly financials to the bank and based on the positive financials (which Myers falsified), he requested an increase to $2.5 million, which the bank granted in 2008. During this time period, Myers was spending a portion of this money on personal items.

Over a three-year period, Myers used the PP National Premium* (NP) credit card to purchase personal items totaling over $750,000. I reviewed each of Myers' credit card purchases, all for personal items. When the NP statement came to the PP office, only Myers was allowed to open the statements. Myers only provided the PP accountant with the first page of the NP statement and ordered the accountant to pay the statement in full each month. The accountant was scared of Myers and afraid of losing his job. The accountant had no knowledge about what was purchased with the NP card, since Myers kept the statement pages detailing the purchases. As PP's funds were drying up, Myers told the accountant what amount to pay on the NP statement and not the full amount. This didn't last much longer as PP was unable to make any of the payments. The NP corporate office contacted one of the PP Board of Directors and asked why payments were not being made on the remaining $100,000 due. The Board members didn't even know that this PP credit card existed. This was the beginning of the end of Myers' employment at PP. As one of the members of the board was on his way to Dallas, Myers was seen shredding documents at the PP office. When the board member arrived, Myers was fired. He blamed everything on the accountant.

What was Myers purchasing with the NP card? He took three vacations on private jets, bringing along family and friends, that cost over $100,000. Myers told his family and friends different stories. The private jet was a PP jet that Myers was allowed to use. Myers told some friends that his annual salary was around $1 million per year. In fact, his annual salary, at the time, was between $150,000 and $175,000. He spent money an expensive country club membership, renovations to his residence, an expensive car, expensive gifts for the family and numerous other personal items. He used this credit card as his personal credit card, but he never paid a dime of it with his own money. What a nice perk to have.

Prior to any knowledge of what Myers was doing at PP, when Myers met with the Board of Directors in California, he fabricated PP's accounts receivables just as he had done with the SEC quarterly reports. This convinced the Board of Directors that PP wasn't on a path of insolvency but was maintaining a steady business. Later, these board members learned that PP was having financial problems and was unable to pay some of the accounts payables (PP's bills). Myers was asked how this was possible with all the accounts receivables coming into PP. They began to wonder if something else was going on. They wanted proof that these were real accounts receivables. Myers created phony PP invoices to indicate that customers of PP owned PP money. Typical of these types of embezzlement cases, the subject tries to hide his actions by falsifying documents. Myers even created a phony letter from a PP customer acknowledging that the customer was aware of their outstanding debt to PP. The amount was listed in this phony letter and the customer would be making a payment soon. These phony PP invoices and this phony customer letter would keep the heat off of Myers for a while. But, like all my white-collar crime cases, the "Sword of Damocles" would in time come unhinged.

The greed and need for money didn't stop here. The accounts payables were piling up inside PP and PP's accountant told Myers that PP was becoming more and more insolvent. Myers found avenues to influx money back into PP. He stopped sending the PP employees' 401K contributions to the third-party company that managed those funds. Instead, the employees 401K contributions were used as PP's operating funds. The employees thought that their 401K funds were growing when in fact they were stagnant. Myers did the same with the PP employees healthcare insurance premium payments, which were automatically deducted from the PP employees' weekly or bi-weekly paychecks. PP employees thought they carried healthcare insurance since their healthcare premiums were being deducted from their paychecks. Unbeknownst to them, their payments were not being sent to the healthcare provider; Myers used these funds to pay the credit card company. Worse, since the employees didn't know they no longer had healthcare insurance, the time elapsed for them to apply for Cobra (Consolidated Omnibus Budget Reconciliation Act). These particular fraudulent acts by Myers added to "jury appeal," should this case make it to trial. I didn't intend for the case to make it to trial, though, since I had plenty of evidence and more to come.

Myers lived in a nice neighborhood in a house that backed up to a golf course and the country club he belonged to. During my investigation, I learned that Myers' next-door neighbor, who had just lost her husband to an illness, was confined to her residence and stricken with terminal cancer. Like a good neighbor, Myers took it upon himself and volunteered to purchase and deliver a few groceries to her. She was happy that he offered. He purchased less than $20 worth of groceries for her and she wrote him a check. He used the information off of her check to gain access via the internet to her account and then began paying his personal bills, like cable, phone, electricity etc., totaling almost $40,000. What are neighbors for? Jury appeal? Absolutely. Myers also asked for a loan from a friend. The friend wrote Myers a check and told him not to worry about paying him back. Instead, Myers used the account number off the check and, using an online program, created blank checks utilizing the account number associated with his friend's bank account. He then wrote checks for over $15,000 to pay personal bills. More "jury appeal."

In late 2011, I flew to California and interviewed a few PP Board members, including the Chairman. Several members of the Board of Directors had invested over $5 million in PP and when Myers drove PP to insolvency, these board members lost their entire investment. The Chairman of the board was one of the wealthiest individuals I had ever interviewed. His investment in PP was approximately $2.5 million. He wasn't happy with what Myers did to PP, but his $2.5 million loss didn't seem to bother him.

In early 2012, I had all the leverage/evidence I needed not only to indict Myers but win a trial case. Again, my goal was to attempt a cold call interview and convince Myers to admit to his scam and plead guilty. In return he would receive a favorable sentence. Again, the decision is left up to the subject who has to ask himself, "Did I commit this crime? Can I win in a trial? Is it worth the risk of losing? How strong is the investigating agent's evidence against me?" I had his residence under loose surveillance with the goal of knowing when he was home, so that I could be prepared to show up in short notice. I received word that Myers was at his residence, but his parents were also there. They were in town visiting. It wasn't a perfect situation, but I was willing to take the risk.

Another agent who was prepared to assist me in this interview was available and ready to go. He was an experienced white-collar crime agent I had worked with for several years and we were also teammates on the Dallas FBI SWAT team. He was also a jokester. You always had to be on your toes with him. We sat within shouting/arguing distance from each other on the squad and he would always rib me that he graduated from a more prestigious university, the University of Texas in Austin and that I had "only" graduated from the University of North Texas in Denton. My comeback was always the same: "We have the same job, title and pay." This didn't deter him from firing away at me. He retired three years prior to my retirement. I hate to say it, but I missed my colleague. Today, we get together often for breakfast and parties. After his retirement, while he was visiting the Frisco RA, he came over to me in the squad area and said, "When you retire all the stress of the job will go away." I responded, "What stress? I don't have or feel any stress." He said, "You will know what I mean when you retire." Jump forward to the day I retired. He was correct. I absolutely knew what he was talking about. What a relaxed feeling even though I loved my job.

Just about every witness and victim told me that Myers would never admit to this fraud and that he was the type of person who has misplaced confidence in himself and could talk his way out of anything. I didn't respond to these comments, but this wasn't my first rodeo and each day I was gathering irrefutable evidence against him.

Normally your partner agent on a subject interview has just general knowledge of your case but is present as a witness and can always ask the subject questions if the opportunity arises. We arrived at Myers' home and knocked on the door. His mother answered, and after identifying who we were, I told her that I wanted to speak to her son. She invited us in. Myers and his dad were sitting at the kitchen table. We identified ourselves and we were invited to sit down. As I explained why we were here I could tell his parents were surprised, but I also had the impression that they thought I was mistaken about their son. They seemed to think I'd just opened this matter and that it was only an inquiry.

When I began asking Myers questions about the PP credit card and the fraudulent invoices, employees' 401Ks and employees' healthcare insurance premiums and other related scams, he blamed the PP accountant, whom I had already interviewed with his Attorney present. I let out a little rope but didn't let him go much further. I had numerous documents in my folder that I was holding that proved all of his fraud.

I told him that numerous witnesses and victims would testify in court against him. I could now see the gravity of the situation expressed on his parents' faces. I sensed that his dad believed me when he stood up and put his hand on Myers' shoulder as if to tell him to tell the truth. I told him he was looking at a lengthy prison sentence (at the time I didn't realize that he was facing over 25 years). I explained the benefit of cooperating and avoiding an indictment and trial. A short time later, as his dad stood over him, he broke down and began to cry. He admitted to all of the scams. His parents were in complete shock.

Later, Myers waived his imminent indictment and pled guilty to one count of Title 18 USC § 1957 (engaging in monetary transactions in property derived from specified unlawful activity). Myers' plea agreement saved him a lot of prison time. If he went to trial and lost, he was looking at a Federal Sentencing Guidelines range of 27 to 33 years in federal prison. Instead, with his plea in 2014, he was sentenced to over nine years in federal prison. Also, he was ordered to pay almost $2 million in restitution. For a rich white-collar criminal, that was a stiff sentence.

As one can imagine, white-collar crime subjects sentenced to federal prison have no real concept of prison life. For the most part they're accustomed to living a rich lifestyle, and to go from that lifestyle to prison must be a jolt. I have only been in two prisons during my career, one state and one federal prison. Let me qualify that—I only visited them for work. I had heard that the federal prisons were luxury compared to the state prisons. The one federal prison I walked through was in Memphis, while I was a member of the Memphis SWAT team. The team was given a tour of the facility, if that is what you want to call it. The other SWAT team members and I were surprised how nice the facilities were. The inmates had an outside workout area with weights, a nice library and landscaped grounds. I thought the landscaping was better than what I had at my residence in Memphis. The state prison was in Texas, and I had to interview an inmate who was a possible witness in a case I was working on. Before I arrived, I read his criminal history and learned that he committed an offense while in prison with only a few months remaining on his sentence. For this offense he was given several more months prison time. I thought, why would you not lay low, keep your nose clean and wait out the few remaining months? I asked him about this. He answered the question nonchalantly. He told me he has spent many years behind bars and his friends were behind these walls and he felt comfortable. He further told me that he didn't have to work, pay bills and had no responsibilities. What a strange, but honest answer. After hearing this madness, I thought maybe we should go back to chain gangs.

High school track team with my long hair.

My disappointed look after finishing 66th in the Texas high school cross-country state meet held in Georgetown, Texas 1979.

Fraternity party: a pimp and his prostitute.

Fraternity party. I think I spent more time putting together costumes than I did studying.

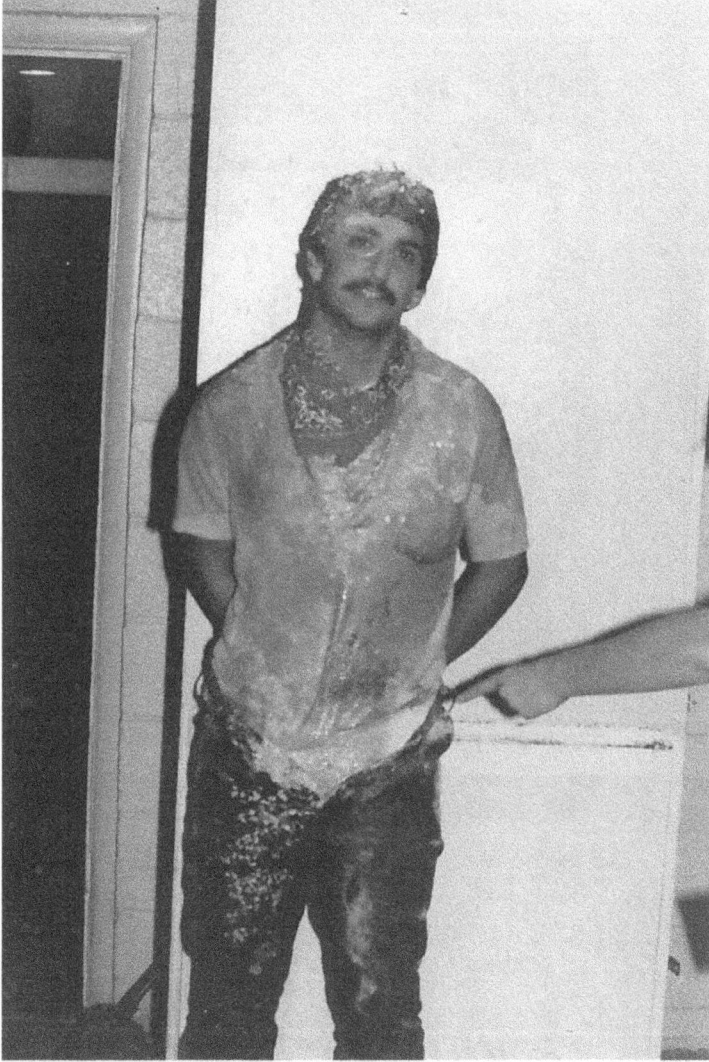

When I was president of the fraternity, I was captured by the pledges from the president's room on the 2nd floor of the fraternity house and thrown over the balcony, taken to a park and trashed. Then the party began. This was a weekly tradition of pledges capturing members, but the president had never been captured before. This was back in the days of hazing.

FBI Academy, 1988

FBI Academy, 1988. Sorry guys, I'm not going to the Board Room, I need to study.

FBI Academy, 1988. Reading my assignment to Memphis, Tennessee to the class.

With my mom at the United States Attorney General's Awards ceremony in Washington DC 2010.

Space Shuttle Columbia debris I found during the shuttle search in East Texas 2003.

Native Americans arriving at our first grid search for the Space Shuttle
Columbia 2003.

Loading up to fly 200 miles northeast of Yellowknife, Northwest Territory, Canada to the Ekati Diamond Mine in the middle of nowhere, 2002.

Flying over the vast tundra heading to Ekati Diamond Mine.

Ekati Diamond Mine.

Rock crusher, Ekati Diamond Mine, 2002

A few dollars' worth of Rough Diamonds – Antwerp, Belgium Diamond District - Diamond School 2003.

SWAT training: marine vessel tactical entry, Mobile, Alabama.

SWAT training with my fully automatic MP5.

SWAT training: room entry tactical training.

SWAT training with Huey Helicopter at Fort Hood, Texas. I'm
seated second from the right.

SWAT training in Houston, Texas preparing for Super Bowl
XXXVIII 2004.

SWAT team standoff with bank robbery, which ended quietly. News
photograph. I'm on the right.

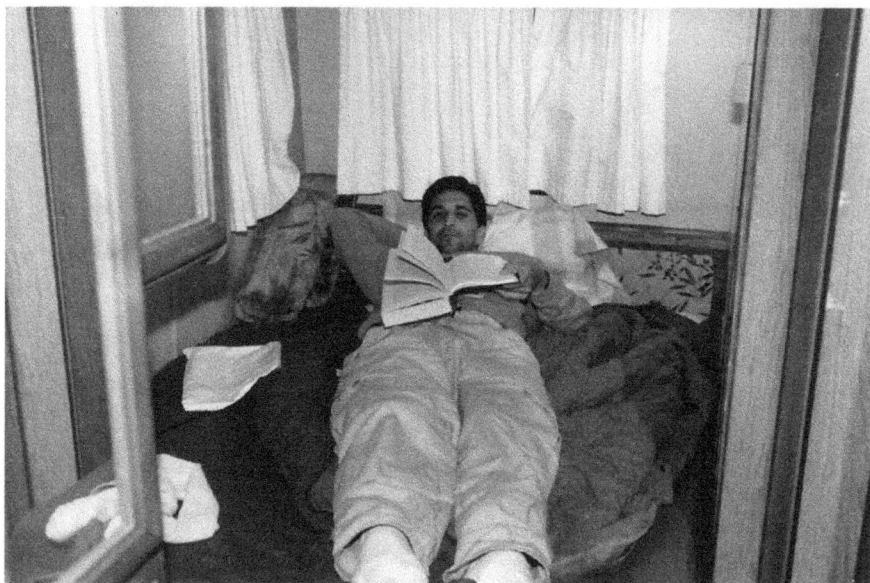

Barely awake in our shack in Jordan. Montana 1996.

SWAT - going on shift in Jordan, Montana 1996.

SWAT team protection detail for the United States Attorney General. I was on the detail for several FBI Directors and United States Attorney Generals, including a criminal Judge from Italy.

Ocoee River, 1996 Olympics Slalom event. Wearing the comical t-shirt uniform. Backpacks hold the collapsible MP5. Note the fanny packs, popular back in the day.

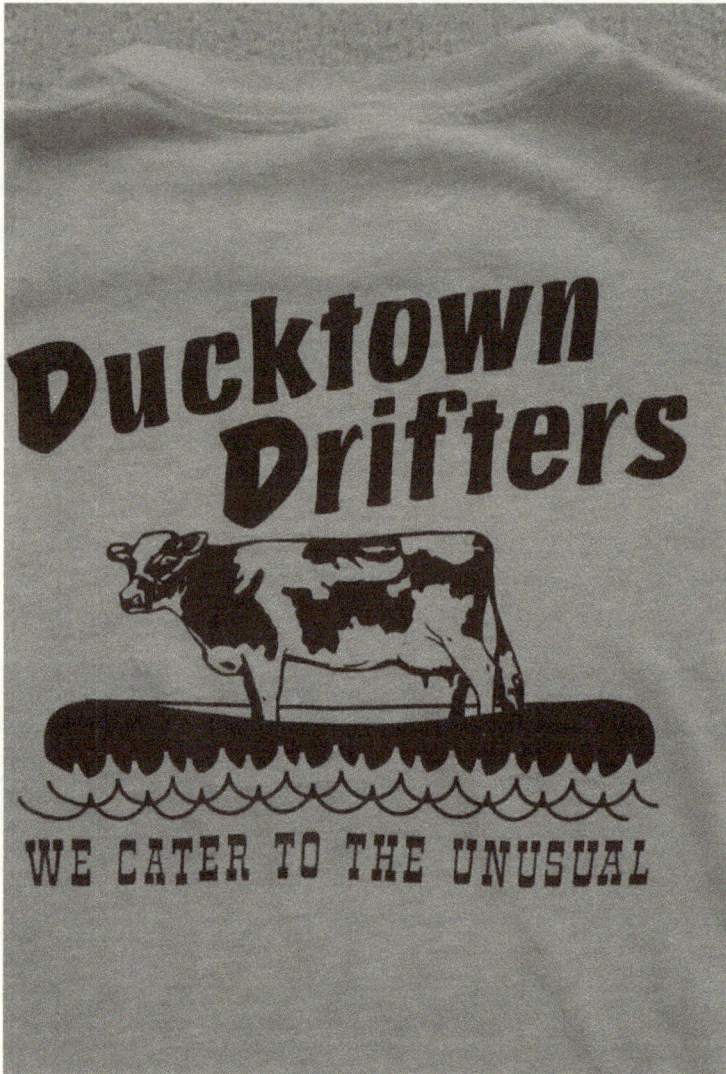

Comical SWAT team t-shirt uniform I wore for the Ocoee River
Slalom event, 1996 Olympics.

1997 photo of L & K Drum Cleaning* with thousands of contaminated 55-gallon drums located in a poor neighborhood in Memphis. This site was an EPA Superfund cleanup and now is covered with green grass and trees.

17

WIND TURBINE SCAM: THE VICTIM'S COMPLAINT

My mandatory retirement clock was ticking, and with my one-year extension, I was now required to retire in August 2019. I wanted to see this case through. I felt as though I was back running my two-mile cross-country race in high school and I needed to kick to the finish.

In early July 2017, while assigned to the Frisco Resident Agency (RA) of the Dallas division, I received information from our Legat office in Canberra, Australia regarding an alleged fraud perpetrated by a 76*-year-old retired United States Army Colonel, Patrick Hamilton*, residing in our AO. The victims were two German citizens, Hauke Von Sauer* and Klaus Wachel*. It's rare that an FBI office would receive information like this from a Legat office that would lead to this type of an investigation. The FBI has offices in over 180 countries covered by 63 Legat offices and 30 sub offices of the Legat offices. We also have 56 field divisions with almost 350 RA offices covering the United States and the United States territories. Over 13,000 FBI agents are scattered amongst these offices.

The "Legat" offices are so named from the term Legal Attaché. The FBI Legat offices work with the law enforcement and security agencies in their host country to coordinate investigations of interest to both countries. The role of Legat is primarily one of coordination, as they don't conduct foreign intelligence gathering or counterintelligence investigations. The rules for joint activities and information sharing are generally spelled out in formal agreements between the United States and the host country.

Typical duties of a Legat include coordinating requests for FBI or host country assistance overseas, conducting investigations in coordination with the host government, sharing investigative leads and information, briefing Embassy counterparts from other agencies, including law enforcement agencies, assessing political and security climates and coordinating victim and humanitarian assistance.

The role Legat Canberra played in this particular case was providing information to the appropriate FBI office, based on the venue of the crime, victim or subject, which occurred in the Dallas Division AO covered by the Frisco RA. Two German citizens, one now living in Australia, Von Sauer, contacted the FBI Legat Canberra and stated that Hamilton defrauded Von Sauer and Wachel out of $2,000,000. They provided only general information to work with and the fact that one victim resided in Germany and the other resided in Australia made it even more difficult to assess.

If a complaint meets the various FBI protocols such as Federal violation, large loss amount, venue etc., an investigation can proceed. For a normal complaint received in the FBI you take the information down, conduct an FBI database search and sit down with the victim(s) to obtain details regarding their complaint. The fact that these victims were German citizens and one was residing in Australia meant that an agent couldn't simply call, email, text or make any type of contact with these foreign citizens without approval from FBI Headquarters, the government of the foreign country in question and informing the Legat office.

This potential case was presented to me by my supervisor, Supervisor Special Agent (SSA) Brandon Lipton*, who knew I was experienced in these types of federal violations. SSA Lipton was the best supervisor I had in 31 years in the FBI. After about 20 years as a street agent (agents who investigate cases or undercover agents), you typically have seniority on your SSA. This was true in my case. If the SSA knows you're an accomplished and successful agent, they respect you and they may also ask you for advice. They will leave you alone to work your cases the way you see fit. SSA Lipton came to me on numerous occasions to ask for my advice, but he also paved many roads for me in my casework. Besides being a great SSA, he was an expert in the cyber field. I had heard he was one of the top, if not the top cyber agent in all of the FBI. What a bonus for someone like myself. I think I had a third grader's level in computer smarts. Okay, I might be exaggerating a bit. It was closer to a first grader's level. SSA Lipton was the go-to person for me with all of my ignorant questions like: how do you turn it on, does it need gas? He always came through, I only understood what the heck he was saying half the time and even wondered if he was actually speaking English. Regardless, he had his expertise and I had mine and we worked well together.

The victim's money was wire transferred from Germany to a bank in the Dallas FBI AO. I told SSA Lipton that I was interested in reviewing the case. We discussed the problem of not being able to interview the victims until approval from FBI Headquarters. So we agreed that I would take another agent and attempt an interview with Hamilton based on the limited information we had. This is the opposite of the steps I would usually take in my investigations. I just didn't attempt to interview a subject until I had fully developed my case and accumulated the necessary evidence. Otherwise, I had no leverage. The subject could simply lie when asked a series of questions, which is a federal violation in itself. This falls under T18 U.S Code §1001—false statements to an FBI agent. And this is exactly what happened.

The basic information I had was whatever Von Sauer had provided to our Legat Canberra office and the Legat provided to the Frisco RA. With a large caseload, it could take one to three years to bring the case to indictment, depending on many factors including the complexity of the case. As you will soon discover, this case grew legs and wings and became more and more complex.

The information Von Sauer and Wachel provided to Legat Cabrera included the following: Von Sauer, Wachel and Hamilton entered into a partnership to build large wind turbines and operate wind turbine farms in Germany. The partnership company was called Wind Energy GmbH* (GmbH is Germany's version of a limited liability company). Von Sauer and Wachel needed €1,355 billion (at the time, approximately $1,550 billion US dollars) to fund this large operation. Hamilton told Von Sauer and Wachel that he owned a company, Worldwide Projects* (WP), which was a group of companies that could provide the loan but required $2 million for a security deposit. The funding would be paid out in three payments between 2015 and 2017. The security deposit would be held in escrow and would be returned at the end of three months plus 20 percent interest

($400,000).

In September 2014, Wachel signed a security deposit loan agreement with Hamilton for the $2 million. The money was transferred from a German bank to Hamilton's bank account in the Dallas AO. In March 2015, Von Sauer signed the €1,355 billion loan agreement with Hamilton.

Von Sauer and Wachel were in constant contact with Hamilton trying to determine why Hamilton hadn't performed on the loans. Well after the three months had elapsed, Hamilton told Von Sauer and Wachel that there was a third party involved who resided in Hong Kong: Larry Kramer*. Kramer was an American citizen who was supposed to fund the loan but hadn't come through. Von Sauer and Wachel hadn't received the return of their security deposit plus the interest nor the €1,355 billion loan for Wind Energy GmbH. Von Sauer and Wachel further advised Legat Canberra that since Von Sauer and Wachel began signing purchase agreement contracts with companies in Germany, Von Sauer's and Wachel's damages had reached over €15 million plus the loss of the security deposit. This was the only information I had for the interview with Hamilton. Not much leverage. With these allegations, I would be investigating possible federal violations of wire fraud, conspiracy and money laundering.

I located an address, which was a motel, for Kramer in McKinney, Texas, a Dallas suburb. SA Don Jasper* and I interviewed one of the motel managers, who vaguely remembered Kramer residing at the motel. But he hadn't resided at the motel for several months. SA Jasper was an experienced white-collar crime agent I had worked with for several years and we were also teammates on the Dallas FBI SWAT team. We remain good friends today. Now it was time to approach Hamilton. I had a good address for Hamilton.

18

WIND TURBINE SCAM: HAMILTON'S INITIAL INTERVIEW

In late July of 2017, SA Jasper* and I traveled to a Dallas suburb to locate and interview Hamilton. The home appeared to have been built in the late 80s or early 90s. It was large, but not elaborate. We knocked on the door and a lady answered. After we identified ourselves by showing her our FBI credentials, we told her we wanted to speak to Mr. Hamilton. She identified herself as his wife. She said he was out of the country on business and should be back today. I handed her my business card and asked her to have her husband call me. The conversation basically ended at that point.

As SA Jasper and I entered my vehicle to depart we both turned to each other and wondered aloud how odd it was that she didn't ask what we wanted with her husband. We certainly expected more than a few questions. "Was he in trouble? Why would the FBI want to speak to my husband?" Anytime I attempted cold call interviews, the person who answered the door asked these types of questions. I would always be vague in my reply, because there was no reason to show my cards. Most people have never met an FBI agent let alone two knocking at their door.

As we were driving back to the office, I received a call from Hamilton who said that he had just landed in Dallas. After I provided basic information about our interest in talking with him, we set up an interview at his home for the next day.

After having a support employee access Hamilton's passport travel information on one of our databases, I was also able to confirm that he had indeed been overseas and had just returned to the United States.

The next day, we were at his home and he was very cordial. His wife was there and she didn't even attempt to sit in on the interview. This too was strange. Most spouses wonder what the heck is going on with their spouse that interests the FBI.

Hamilton stated that WP operates four companies with offices all over the United States and worldwide and that he had over 20 employees working overseas (this was not true). He further explained that WP had been in business for several years and conducted humanitarian work outside the United States by managing and assisting in the construction of projects such as hospitals, housing and roads.

Hamilton met Von Sauer 10 years ago in Asia. Hamilton traveled to Germany and met with Von Sauer and Wachel to discuss the wind turbine partnership. They agreed to purchase wind turbine parts and have the wind turbines built in Germany with an estimated cost of $500 million. One of Hamilton's WP companies would fund this project, but Hamilton required a security deposit of $2 million. Once Hamilton funded the project he would own 60 percent of Wind Energy GmbH until the loan was paid back. Once the loan was paid back, Hamilton's ownership would drop to 40 percent. Later, and after the fact, Von Sauer and Wachel learned that Hamilton invested the $2 million with Kramer. (I later learned that Hamilton didn't inform Von Sauer and Wachel about Kramer until several months later.) Kramer resided in Hong Kong, but had an office in Plano, Texas. Hamilton's signed contract with Kramer stated that Kramer would return $100 million in three months.

Hamilton furnished a copy of this contract to me during the interview. Hamilton stated that in September 2014, Von Sauer and Wachel sent four wire transfers to Hamilton's Dallas area bank account and Hamilton immediately wire transferred this money to Kramer's Dallas area bank account.

The purpose of sending Von Sauer and Wachel's $2 million to Kramer, was that Kramer would invest this money in a currency exchange (a common scam) in Hong Kong. In about 100 days, Kramer expected to return between $75 million and $100 million. This money would be used towards the loan for Wind Energy GmbH. Hamilton explained that Kramer had conducted billions of dollars in currency exchanges.

I asked for documentation to support this, but Hamilton couldn't provide any. When I asked Hamilton if he had ever invested with Kramer before, Hamilton said that approximately 10 years earlier, Hamilton invested $2 to $5 million with Kramer. After a few months, Kramer, through these currency exchanges, returned $75 million to Hamilton. (This was a false statement in violation of Title 18 USC §1001.) Now mind you, Hamilton was a retired Army Colonel. Again, I asked him for documentation and he had nothing to provide. I asked him what he did with the $75 million and he said he invested it in his WP companies.

During this interview. I'm jokingly asking myself; *how can I invest in this currency exchange?* I couldn't grasp that Hamilton seriously believed that SA Jasper and I would believe this. It was like Hamilton thought we'd just fallen off a turnip truck. Hamilton mentioned a third party, Bobby Fletcher* located in Vermont*, who was also working with Hamilton and Kramer. Hamilton said he had daily contact with Fletcher and Kramer and blamed all of these problems on Kramer but assured us that Kramer would come through with the money. Since I had no evidence to prove Hamilton wrong, we ended the interview. But both of us knew there was a case here.

A short time later, I was able to establish the venue of the fraud, which occurred in the Eastern District of Texas (EDTX) with the banks used by Hamilton and Kramer. I contacted my favorite AUSA in the EDTX, Tim Garrett*. He was just a short 15 minutes away in an office in Plano, Texas. I explained the allegations and that the fraud occurred in the EDTX. As usual, AUSA Garrett was all in, telling me to keep him in the loop and let him know if I needed anything. I was always comfortable working with AUSA Garrett. He was very detailed, almost too detailed, but it kept me focused on the smallest things, which kept me on the correct path.

One week later I officially opened an investigation, which led me traveling to Frankfurt, Germany, Vermont, Miami, Washington DC and Los Angeles, chasing leads and potential subjects.

19

---•◦•---

WIND TURBINE SCAM: VICTIMS INTERVIEWED IN GERMANY

Prior to my departure to Frankfurt to interview Von Sauer and Wachel, I subpoenaed Hamilton's and Kramer's bank records.

As I have mentioned, personal interviews of the victim(s) in my cases were essential to solving them. The only option I had was to travel to Frankfurt and interview Von Sauer and Wachel. This was not as simple as it may sound. I can't simply contact Von Sauer and Wachel and say, "Let's meet. I'll hop on a plane and see you soon." I have to follow FBI and State Department rules and policies and obtain official clearance to conduct interviews of foreign citizens on foreign land. I also need to be tracked by the FBI for safety reasons. I understood all of this, but that was a lot of red tape that could slow down an investigation.

When I travel to Europe for vacation, there's far less red tape, though I'm still required to be briefed before I leave and when I return. Even when I'm not on official FBI business, I could end up in a ditch with a beer mug cracked over my head or be kidnapped. But I do understand the purpose of these rules.

I only asked for approval to speak to Von Sauer. I received this approval, which was fine, especially since Von Sauer spoke very good English and Wachel spoke little English.

During this time period, I had opened another case on a completely different matter, and my victim, Melvin Martin* was located in London and my subject had homes in East Texas and Switzerland. I bring this up because the timing was perfect. I was able to conduct an interview with Martin in London and then travel to Frankfurt to interview Von Sauer and Wachel. I was being resourceful. I was prepared to conduct these interviews alone, but SSA Lipton suggested I pick another agent to travel with me. The choice was easy. I would ask SA Jasper, since he assisted on the original interview of Hamilton and he was the number two senior agent on the squad, myself being the most senior agent.

SA Jasper was all in. We had countless paperwork to fill out and submit to FBI Headquarters in order to receive our approvals to travel and conduct FBI investigations in foreign countries. We both spent a full day getting this paperwork done.

We first traveled to London and met Martin at his office. He had a good sense of humor and had just survived a serious illness. He was also defrauded out of approximately $2 million by a United States citizen. Also present as required in the interview was a London Bobby. He was a quiet man, but very nice. I think he was overwhelmed with what he heard in the interview. During a break I asked him what type of firearm he carried. He said he didn't carry a firearm and that most London Bobbies didn't. I asked what he would do if he ran into a situation that would require a firearm. He said he would call it in and the Bobbies who carried firearms would take care of it. How different things were in London.

I pulled out a Dallas FBI coffee mug from a sack I was carrying and handed to him as a gift. He thanked me. I was certain he would drink tea out of it.

We took a lunch break and Martin offered to buy us lunch and a couple of beers, but we turned him down. The FBI is strict on things like this, and I totally agree with this policy. We are supposed to be the pinnacle of law enforcement worldwide. He thanked us for being professional. Our all-day interview with Martin was successful.

The next day SA Jasper and I had lunch at a nice restaurant in London. We enjoyed people watching, but we noticed that Londoners dressed in their business suits were downing beers as if it was water. This wasn't a norm in the United States during business hours. Then again, the FBI is strict about such things, as people would and should assume. A well-known phrase in the FBI is DEB - "Don't Embarrass the Bureau." We're not perfect and have had our disappointments, but hopefully we will remain that pinnacle.

That evening as we were in the hotel elevator on our way to a local pub to have dinner and drinks, the elevator door opened and four attractive young women entered the elevator laughing and cutting up. Some were wearing Baltimore Ravens tops. They were Ravens cheerleaders in town for an NFL game in London. Being a huge Dallas Cowboys fan, I turned to them and asked if they were Dallas Cowboys cheerleaders. I didn't even get a laugh or comment. Maybe they were jealous. Early Friday morning, we flew to Frankfurt to interview Von Sauer and Wachel.

We arrived early and met with Von Sauer and Wachel at an undisclosed United States controlled location and spent all day interviewing them. When needed, Von Sauer translated our questions for Wachel and Wachel's answers to our questions. Von Sauer and Wachel were likable, easy to speak with and professional businessmen. They were experienced and successful in the wind turbine business in Germany and other countries.

Ten years prior, Von Sauer had met Hamilton in Asia and Hamilton told Von Sauer that he was interested in investing in renewable energy. Hamilton told Von Sauer and Wachel that five wealthy Dallas families had established the funding for WP. (In my second interview with Hamilton, he couldn't confirm or provide evidence to the existence of these five wealthy families.) Hamilton had previously provided them with a board minutes document supporting this claim, which appeared to be registered and stamped in the state of Texas. This board meeting document was signed by Margret Wilkens*. (Later, I located and interviewed Wilkens. She said that her deceased father and Hamilton had worked together at a large company in Dallas during the early 1990s. She had typed up these minutes as a favor to Hamilton and filed it with the state of Texas. She didn't know what type of business WP was and described Hamilton as a blowhard.)

In 2014, Von Sauer and Hamilton began discussing in detail a partnership which now included Wachel, and they later met in Germany to discuss the details. Prior to any money being exchanged, Hamilton presented Von Sauer and Wachel with Hamilton's WP presentation document, which included all four WP companies. The presentation document included the corporate organizational structure, a map showing office locations in the United States and worldwide and joint projects completed and under construction worldwide. None of these projects were in the United States. The numerous construction projects included: an apartment complex, hospital, petroleum refinery, mine, airport, stadium, food plant, power plant and other projects, all in foreign countries. Also included in the presentation document were pictures, which appeared to be current or completed projects. This document was several pages long and Von Sauer and Wachel were impressed with it. Von Sauer later provided me with the presentation document.

According to Von Sauer and Wachel, this helped convince them of Hamilton's ability to loan the funds for the wind turbine project. Hamilton then told Von Sauer and Wachel about the $2 million security deposit to be held in escrow for 100 days in order for Hamilton's company to loan $256 million for the wind turbine project. Hamilton was explicit that the security deposit remain in an escrow account with a return of the $2 millions plus $400,000 in interest. There was no mention of a third party. Von Sauer conducted very little due diligence on Hamilton and the WP companies. There just wasn't much information available.

They trusted him. Hamilton talked a good game and appeared to be very successful in other projects. Plus, he was a retired United States Army Colonel, which added credibility. Von Sauer and Wachel would arrange purchases of parts, equipment and land in Germany. These purchases would require Von Sauer and/or Wachel to sign legally binding purchase agreements. Hamilton's name wouldn't be on any of the agreements. Von Sauer and Wachel would be setting themselves up for financial ruin if Hamilton's loan didn't come through. In September 2014, Wachel signed the $2 million loan agreement with Hamilton. A few days later, Von Sauer and Wachel made four wire transfers totaling $2 million from a bank in Germany to Hamilton's Dallas area bank.

The beginning of Von Sauer and Wachel's financial ruin was now in motion with much more to come. Von Sauer and Wachel began negotiating with various wind turbine related companies in Germany. Since contracts needed to be drawn up, Von Sauer and Wachel hired a German law firm to draft the contracts. Von Sauer and Wachel agreed to pay the law firm $40,000. Wachel also hired an accounting firm for $200,000 to write a contract to purchase another wind turbine business. Wachel was reluctant to sign contracts to purchase any of these companies unless Hamilton produced the funding. But each time he asked about the funding, Hamilton would convince him that the money would be there any day. Hamilton adamantly stated that the $2 million plus interest, and more importantly the large loan, would be coming through any day. By now the amount of funds required to make the necessary purchases had reached €1,355 billion (approximately $1,550 billion USD) and Hamilton assured Von Sauer and Wachel that WP would lend this amount of money.

During this interview I was thinking to myself, "No, no. Stop guys!"

After hearing all the lies Hamilton was feeding Von Sauer and Wachel, I inadvertently said "This is bullshit." Wachel slowly repeated the word, as if asking what is this word? The rest of us laughed. Von Sauer turned to Wachel and translated what bullshit meant in German. I was happy to get a smile out of Wachel, because most of the interview he appeared to be very concerned about what had happened. Wachel was a wealthy man, but his financial life was only going to get worse.

Hamilton's emails to Von Sauer and Wachel continually stated that the money was coming tomorrow. And each day when tomorrow came, Hamilton would state in another email that the money would come tomorrow. SA Jasper made the comment, "Free crab tomorrow." I whispered to SA Jasper and asked what he meant. He whispered back, "Don't you know the 'Free crab tomorrow' signs on the walls at Joe's Crab Shack restaurants?" I hadn't heard about those signs, but I could see how they related now.

By the end of January/early February 2015, Von Sauer and Wachel had become very concerned, since they had signed purchase contracts with German companies and Hamilton had not funded the loan nor paid back the $2 million plus interest. Around March 2015, the concern became a panic when Hamilton admitted that he invested the money with a man named Larry Kramer. The money was not in an escrow account as promised earlier. Hamilton assured Von Sauer and Wachel that Kramer would be wiring the money soon. Von Sauer and Wachel would have never agreed to this had Hamilton been up front with them.

Hamilton told them that the money was invested in a Chinese currency exchange. He never mentioned to Von Sauer and Wachel that he had invested money with Kramer in the past. Von Sauer and Wachel questioned Hamilton about Kramer and he was evasive and reluctant to provide any information, only that he had met Kramer several years earlier. Hamilton would not provide any contact information for Kramer, but Hamilton's contact with Kramer is almost exclusively through Kramer's attorney, Bob* located in the northeast part of the United States. Hamilton claimed that he didn't know Bob's last name. In my investigation, prior to my interview of Von Sauer and Wachel, I came across a name associated with Kramer, Bob Fletcher* located in Vermont*. I asked Von Sauer if this was the Bob that Von Sauer was referring to. He said that sounded correct.

I could easily list over 50 excuses Hamilton told Von Sauer and Wachel as to why the money had not arrived. Some were truly absurd. Here are just a few: the money has to transfer through Hamilton's accountant located in New Zealand which takes 45 days; the currency money exchange is being reviewed by the Chinese government; the United States customs had placed a hold on the money, New York lawyers have to sign release documents; courts in New York have to clear the money; the money has been transferred to a bank in Argentina but is on the way; the money had been seized but should clear any day. Hamilton gave these excuses through email and Skype messages. There were hundreds of emails and Skype messages. Each email and Skype misrepresentation was subject to wire fraud charges in furtherance of the scheme.

At the time of our interview, Wachel's losses exceeded $5.5 million. He had borrowed almost $2 million from his private company's pension fund and the money was due back with mounting interest fees (and later lawsuits). Wachel was beginning to be sued by the German companies he signed purchase agreements with. His world was beginning to downward spiral. Here was a successful and wealthy businessman who had an esteemed reputation in the wind turbine industry but was about to be destroyed and discredited.

Our interview of Von Sauer and Wachel took nearly an entire day. Because I had clearance, I knew I could contact Von Sauer with follow up questions when I returned to the United States. But once I returned, I didn't have clearance to contact Wachel. Von Sauer and Wachel's biggest concern was getting their money back, not sending Hamilton to federal prison, which is understandable. Von Sauer even asked, "How can Hamilton pay the money back if he is sitting in prison and not generating income?" But for agents of the FBI, the prosecution of federal crimes is the goal. I explained this to them and added that if and when this gets to the sentencing phase, the federal judge usually orders the defendant to pay restitution. I also explained the harsh reality that more times than not the defendant had already spent the stolen money. We concluded the interview.

The next day, SA Jasper traveled to Stuttgart, Germany to do a little touring and I hopped on a train and headed to a small town in the Netherlands to visit some good friends. I stayed with them at their beautiful home, which I have visited several times in the past, and on Monday I flew out of Amsterdam and back to Dallas.

.

20

——◈·◈——

WIND TURBINE SCAM: TRAVEL TO VERMONT

When I returned to the Frisco RA I reviewed the subpoenaed Hamilton bank records, which included the wire transfers from Von Sauer and Wachel in Germany to Hamilton's account. I had Kramer's bank records, too, which included Hamilton's wire transfers to Kramer's account. As Hamilton began receiving the wire transfers from Von Sauer and Wachel, he immediately began wire transferring these funds to Kramer. What was disturbing was that as soon as Kramer received the wire transfers from Hamilton, he immediately wire-transferred funds totaling $1 million to individuals located in China. (These must have been the individuals Kramer owed money to in China, which is what Fletcher told me in a later interview.). Even more disturbing, Kramer wire transferred $1 million to Michael Morgan* in San Clemente, California. Almost 20 years prior, the Portland FBI office had a case with Morgan and Kramer titled as the subjects of a similar $2 million fraud case. In that case, Morgan was indicted, arrested, pled guilty and spent a few years in federal prison. Morgan's prison time didn't seem to slow him down. I would later attempt to interview him as my retirement sandglass clock was running out. Another rabbit hole to run down with more to come.

Shortly after I returned to the Frisco RA, I began tracking down Bobby Fletcher* in Vermont*. I located what I thought was a good address and made contact with the FBI division that covers Vermont. After receiving travel approval from SSA Lipton and the ASAC, the

131

ASAC jokingly said, "Hey Kamel I know this isn't a travel boondoggle. Who travels to Vermont in late January?" I hadn't thought about what the weather might be like in Vermont in late January. But he had confidence in me, and he had no issues with me taking this trip whether it was successful or not.

I contacted the FBI to have a local agent meet me at the airport and we would travel to Fletcher's residence to attempt a cold call interview. I arrived in Vermont in late January 2018. The agent assigned to assist me was sharp and motivated to assist. As soon as he picked me up, he looked at my clothes and jokingly said, "You're going to stand out in small town Vermont." I was wearing slacks, a button up shirt and one of my Lombardo jackets to conceal my weapon.

My plan was to surveil the residence before we made our approach. We drove about 45 minutes through the beautiful, snow-covered countryside. So many of these cold call interviews can fail whether you do your due diligence or not. But it's important to maximize your chances that your subject will be home.

During my career, I had been successful locating and interviewing a subject or potential subject about 90 percent of the time with cold calls. Maybe that was just luck.

On one occasion, I attempted to conduct a cold call interview of a potential subject in New York City. I thought I had a good address. I was meeting two Department of Justice (DOJ) attorneys who were flying in from another location. I arrived late at night, checked into my hotel and crashed. The next morning I met with the two DOJ Attorneys at breakfast. After breakfast, we took a short cab ride to the residence, which was in a high-rise building with a nicely dressed doorman standing outside. I identified myself, told him who I was here to see, and he told me that this person had moved out a few months prior. So basically, I flew to New York City, had breakfast and boarded the next flight back to Dallas.

Okay, I'll mention another one that was unexpectedly successful. In the early 2000s, prior to Google Maps, I had a Chicago address for an important witness in a case. I also had a few back up addresses. I flew to Chicago with a DOJ Attorney. We planned to conduct this interview and fly back early the next morning. The sun was setting when we arrived at the main address and knocked on the door. The man who answered the door said that he had moved into this residence about a month ago and the person I was looking for had moved out. I asked if he had his new address and he said that the subject had moved across the border into Wisconsin. I thanked him and sat in the car with the DOJ attorney. One of the backup addresses in my list was in a small Wisconsin town just across the border. The DOJ Attorney said it was getting late and mentioned that we didn't have a map of this town, so how could we locate the address? I suggested we give it a shot anyway. I knew the town was small and felt confident we could find the street. He thought I was crazy, but as we entered the town I saw the street immediately and we continued on to the address. It was late at night, but we saw lights on in the residence and vehicles in the driveway. We knocked on the door and were happily surprised that he was there. He invited us in, and I apologized for coming by so late. He was very gracious.

We arrived at the address I had for Fletcher and set up a few hundred yards away to watch for movement. There was one car in the driveway, but for about 45 minutes we didn't see any activity. Then a woman came out of the residence with a dog and she walked right past us. After about 15 minutes, we saw her walking back by our car. I told my partner to drive up just as she was getting in the driveway, and we would approach her. We drove up, exited the vehicle, identified ourselves with our FBI credentials and told her who we wanted to speak to. She said that Fletcher was her father. I told her that he wasn't in any trouble (which wasn't exactly true) and that we merely wanted to speak to him. She said he was inside and as she walked into the garage, I was right behind her.

As she pushed open the door to the residence, I didn't let the door close and continued walking right behind her. She headed up the stairs that led from the garage inside to the residence. She paused for just a second on the stairs and looked back at us. Then she continued and so did we.

She said, "Dad, there are some people here to see you." As we topped the stairs, we had our credentials out and identified ourselves to Fletcher. He was startled, but that's completely normal when someone is unexpectedly approached by FBI agents, especially inside their residence.

Let me make a comment on FBI agents presenting their credentials. This is a very important policy, and it should be. If someone approaches you and tells you he or she is an FBI agent and wants to speak to you and they don't present their credentials, something is wrong. Ask to see them. If you have seen the movie *A Simple Plan*, you will understand the importance of this. Now, on a handful of occasions, I have had people say, "How do they know those are real FBI credentials?" That's a good question. Once, while I was assigned to the Memphis FBI office, I was alone when I knocked on the door of a potential witness in one of my cases. I was dressed in my suit. A lady with a telephone up against her ear opened the curtain of the dining room window and looked at me. I presented my credentials through the window and she put one finger up signaling one minute, then closed the curtain. I waited for the door to open, but after a few minutes I knocked again. Again, she opened the curtain and put one finger up, then closed the curtain. I figured it out and I turned around towards the street and waited. A few minutes later, a Memphis police squad car pulled into the driveway and I showed the officer my credentials as the lady exited the residence. The police officer told her I was legitimate and she invited me in. She apologized and I told her she did the right thing.

Fletcher invited us to sit. I explained that I was from the Dallas Division of the FBI, and I wanted to ask him questions regarding his association with Hamilton and Kramer. He acknowledged that he knew them, and that he partially worked for Hamilton. Hamilton would pay Fletcher a 5 percent commission for finding investors. But Fletcher never earned a single commission. Fletcher showed me a vague, one-page commission contract. He said he spoke to Hamilton and Kramer almost daily. Ernie Rutgers* had introduced Fletcher to Hamilton by telephone but had never met Hamilton in person. Fletcher met Kramer through Henry Long*, a long-time associate located in California. Long and Kramer had worked together on some type of oil venture in the past.

Fletcher and Hamilton communicated mostly by email and telephone. According to Fletcher, Hamilton had projects all over the world. He told Fletcher that he had a client in China who was interested in funding 2 million Chinese Renminbis for seed money in a project. Hamilton wanted to exchange the 2 million Renminbis for American or Hong Kong dollars. Hamilton asked Fletcher if he knew anyone in China who could exchange this money. That's when Fletcher contacted Kramer in Hong Kong. Kramer told Fletcher that he could exchange $2 million with a return of $100 million, but this was a one-time deal. But for whatever reason, the Chinese client backed out.

Sometime later, even though the deal with the Chinese client fell through, Hamilton asked Fletcher if Kramer could still do the currency exchange. Hamilton told Fetcher that Hamilton had $2 million to invest. Hamilton didn't tell Fletcher where this money came from (it was Von Sauer and Wachel's security deposit to be held in escrow). According to Fletcher, Kramer said that he could only exchange $1 million, maybe $1.5 million. Hamilton was firm that it must be $2 million. Kramer said yes to the $2 million and Kramer would return $100 million to Hamilton in 90 days. Kramer also told Fletcher that he owed someone in China $1 million. (This lined up with my review of Kramer's wire transfers.)

Well after the 90 days, Fletcher tried to get Kramer to pay Hamilton the $100 million. He said that he was familiar with a wind turbine investment, but what Hamilton was doing didn't make sense.

I asked Fletcher how much money he received in this transaction. Fletcher didn't know what I did or didn't know about his finances, bank accounts etc. He said that during this time period, Fletcher received a $300,000 wire transfer from Kramer, but this was considered a loan. I asked for the contract and or loan agreement. Fletcher had nothing to show for it. He said the loan was a verbal agreement. I thought my partner was going to come out of his seat when he heard this. We told Fletcher that what he just said sounded very suspicious and I promised to follow up with this information. I was thinking to myself, "Sure Fletcher, and I have some land just West of San Diego to sell." Another rabbit hole to pursue.

Fletcher said that he didn't have an exact address for Kramer in Hong Kong. When I returned to Dallas, I called Fletcher and told him in no uncertain terms that the $300,000 he received from Kramer was somehow involved in this fraud. I told Fletcher he was not the "big fish" in my investigation, but that he must provide updated information on Hamilton and Kramer's activities and, most importantly, locate an address for Kramer in Hong Kong. I could tell Fletcher was very happy to hear this from me. He came through with information, and later a location for Kramer in Hong Kong.

Prior to obtaining a Hong Kong address for Kramer, I had reached out to our office in Hong Kong and spoke to an Assistant Legal

Attaché (ALAT). ALATs are agents in our Legat offices. I told him that I was trying to locate Kramer. Surprisingly, he told me once I obtained an address for Kramer, to send him a lead with questions so he could interview him. I had been around the block long enough to know this couldn't be done. A few months later, Fletcher came through with an address, but it was a temporary address. I jumped on my fast horse and contacted the ALAT in Hong Kong. To my disappointment, but not my surprise, he told me he couldn't do this interview. We needed to involve the Hong Kong authorities, to which I basically replied, "Forget it." What a waste of my time.

21

WIND TURBINE SCAM: NIGERIAN
AND BULGARIAN VICTIMS

A short time later in early 2018, I received a call at my desk from an agent in the Los Angeles FBI office. He asked if I had a case on Patrick Hamilton? He told me he just interviewed a walk-in complaint from Eniola Choji*, of Nigeria. Choji told him that Hamilton had defrauded him out of $1.6 million in 2012. After the agent interviewed Choji, he did his due diligence and entered Hamilton's name into the FBI database and received a hit on my open case. My FBI career was closing in on 30 years and I couldn't tell you how many times I had received complaint calls about scams operated by Nigerians out of Nigeria. It was common knowledge. Luckily for the FBI, these scams are mostly handled by the United States Secret Service. But for me to hear that a Nigerian citizen was scammed by an American citizen was bizarre. Almost funny.

The Los Angeles agent forwarded the Choji's interview to me. Before I received the FD-302 (these are our forms used to memorize reports of our interviews), I contacted Choji in a rare telephone interview. He was currently residing in Los Angeles and trying to locate his $1.6 million. In 2012, Choji was a Nigerian Tribal Chief, a well-respected position in Nigeria. He was a wealthy businessman and was working with a small group of Nigerians seeking to raise $150 million to construct a shopping mall in Nigeria. Through a third party in Nigeria, Choji was introduced to Hamilton by telephone. Hamilton told Choji that his company could loan the $150 million, but Hamilton required a security deposit of $1.6 million, which would be held in an escrow account for 90 days. Sound familiar? Yet another rabbit hole.

To help sell Hamilton's ability to fund the project, Hamilton told Choji about completed WP projects and current WP projects being funded by WP, sharing photographs of these projects to bolster his claims. Hamilton also told Choji that he could obtain funds from the church Hamilton attends. The church funds humanitarian projects and has up to $2 billion to fund projects all over the world. How crazy is this?

Even knowing what the results would be, I set up an interview with the pastor of this megachurch. As expected, he told me that the church doesn't fund projects and it definitely doesn't have $2 billion sitting around. The church was barely getting by financially.

Choji was sold on Hamilton's misrepresentations and relayed this information to the other Nigerian partners. In 2014, a contract was signed between Choji and Hamilton, which covered the funding amount, the security deposit and the fact that the money would be held in an escrow account for 90 days. The contract also stated that the $150 million would be made available at the end of 90 days. Choji furnished $600,000 out of his pocket and the other Nigerians came up with the remaining $1 million. The money was wire transferred through a Los Angeles bank to Westcoast Escrow Company* (WEC) also located in Los Angeles. The account was in Hamilton's name. At the time, Choji didn't know that he didn't have signature authority nor access to the account.

After the funding due date passed, Choji began asking Hamilton about the escrow money and the $150 million loan. Hamilton gave Choji several different excuses (again, see a pattern here?) as to why the funding wasn't available. Choji passed these ridiculous excuses on to the other Nigerian investors. This continued through 2014, and understandably, the other Nigerian investors didn't believe Choji, nor did they care. They just wanted their $1 million back. In the later part of 2014, the other investors went to the Nigerian authorities. The authorities told Choji that he had two months to return the $1 million to the investors. Choji was already out $600,000, and he didn't have $1 million to pay the other investors. Choji was truly in a panic. Not only did he want to recover his $600,000, but he also didn't want to go to prison. But in January 2015, Choji was arrested and sentenced to two years in prison. Can you imagine one day you are the Chief of your

Nigerian Tribe, well respected, planning to build a shopping mall for your community, then the next moment you lose $600,000 of your own money in a scam, then sent to prison for two years? I have seen many scam victims wiped out financially, but none of them had salt poured on their wounds by going to prison.

Let me make some comments about continuing down this long and winding road in the Choji matter. The fraud occurred in 2014 and continued into early 2015. The federal violation of wire fraud has a five-year statute of limitations, which ends five years after the last offense. My window for indictment in the Choji matter was closing soon. But I still had time in the wind turbine scam, since Hamilton continued the scam through his Skype and other wire communications with Von Sauer and Wachel, even up until indictment.

I obtained numerous documents from Choji, including the contract he had signed with Hamilton, and subpoenaed the Los Angeles bank and WEC for the escrow account records. Hamilton had an account set up at WEC and he was the only individual who had signature authority on the account. A short time after the $1.6 million arrived in Hamilton's WEC escrow account, I noticed several email/letter requests sent to WEC's owner to transfer funds to five individuals' and companies' bank accounts located throughout the United States. The letters had Hamilton's signature. The transfer amounts ranged from $3,500 to almost $1.2 million. Each transfer was another lead and another rabbit hole. Who were these individuals and companies? What connection did they have with Hamilton? Why were they receiving this money? Too much to investigate with too little time.

These wire transfers from Hamilton's escrow account were requested by email and were accompanied by a letter that appeared to be signed by Hamilton. I began comparing these wire transfer requests. What didn't jump out at me the first few times I studied the letters were Hamilton's signatures. Hamilton had a partner in this investment, "Big" Earl Roper*. Roper must have had access to the WEC escrow account, because he introduced Hamilton to the owner of WEC, Linda Koda*.

One day I had all the documents Choji turned over to me and the subpoenaed Hamilton escrow account records from WEC spread out over our large conference room table in the Frisco RA. I did this often in the conference room. It was my go-to place to spread out my evidence. I was trying to piece the puzzle together. As I was sorting through the wire transfers and comparing them to the WP letter transfer requests with Hamilton's signature, something caught my eye. I kept staring at Hamilton's signature on the letters. Then it hit me. These weren't handwritten signatures. They were identical, most likely e-signatures (electronic signatures) or possibly stamp signatures. Hamilton's signatures could easily be added to these letters. But who added them? Was it Hamilton? Since Roper had been connected Koda at WEC, could he have played a part in these signatures? I needed to present these letters to Hamilton and Roper and ask these questions.

I had been going back and forth investigating the German wind turbine scam and the Nigerian shopping mall scam, when in April 2019, I received a telephone call from a DOJ Attorney in Washington DC. The DOJ Attorney told me that he had received information from an Attorney (also the victim), Boiko Golakov*, who was located in Bulgaria, and his Washington DC Attorney regarding Hamilton defrauding him out of millions of dollars. Now more than ever, there were too many rabbit holes to chase down. My stress level was mounting. I was hesitant to meet on this matter, because I knew I would be even more overwhelmed. At the DOJ Attorney's urging, I agreed to meet with the DOJ Attorney, the local Washington Attorney and Golakov in Washington DC. The DOJ Attorney told me that Golakov spoke little English, but in the meeting there would also be a DOJ-contracted employee who spoke Bulgarian and would translate. The Washington DC Attorney representing Golakov also spoke Bulgarian and she would assist in translating when needed.

In late April 2019, I flew to Washington D.C. My hotel was within walking distance of the DOJ office where the interview would take place. First, I was to meet with the DOJ contracted translator in the lobby of the DOJ office. I'm usually good with directions, even without Google Maps, but damned if I could find this DOJ office. I was wearing a nice suit and walked and walked in circles trying to find the building. I even had the translator on the phone. It was like I was walking blind. He had to guide me to the building. It was definitely nondescript. I finally found the building and walked into the lobby. I sat down and visited with the translator and we waited for what seemed like a long time to get someone to take us through all the security points.

Present in this interview/meeting were myself, the DOJ Attorney, Golakov, the Washington DC Attorney and the DOJ contracted translator. Golakov was clearly upset with allegedly being defrauded out of millions of dollars. The translation process slowed the progress of the interview, but I soon learned that Golakov had partnered on a project with Hamilton in Bulgaria. After well over an hour and a half into the interview, Golakov said, through the translator, that he partnered with Hamilton mainly as his Attorney. I couldn't believe what I was hearing, so, I asked the translator to ask Golakov to repeat what he had just said. Golakov repeated that he was Hamilton's attorney during the partnership. At that point I turned to the DOJ Attorney and said, "We need to stop the interview." I asked the DOJ attorney and the Washington DC attorney to step out in the hall. We left the conference room and walked to the break room.

I asked the DOJ Attorney, "Did you know about this"? He said this was the first time he had heard it. I said, "I think we have a problem with attorney-client privilege and I'm not comfortable continuing the interview." The DOJ attorney immediately agreed. Golakov's Washington DC attorney tried to argue that the attorney-client privileges were different in Bulgaria and that it would be fine to continue the interview. I quietly called "bullshit" but didn't use that word. Instead, I told her that since we are in the United States and this is an FBI case, we can't use the laws of Bulgaria in this matter. We were on a slippery slope. She said it would be difficult for Golakov to travel back to the United States. So after our 15-minute meeting in the break room, we agreed to stop the interview. I told the DOJ attorney that it would help if he called the AUSA in this case and I provided him with the contact number. We walked back into the conference room where it was announced that the interview would not continue. Golakov was irate. I'm glad I didn't understand Bulgarian at the time. He went on and on as I was gathering my documents. I apologized as much as I could, thanked the translator and we walked out together. This was mostly a waste of time, but I had a nice dinner sitting outside that night and flew back to Dallas the next morning. This was not a beneficial interview, but I knew I had prevented a potentially enormous problem.

22

<hr/>

WIND TURBINE SCAM: YOUR MONEY IS GONE

I reviewed both of Hamilton's contracts, one with Wachel (the $2 million security deposit) and one contract with Von Sauer (€1,355 billion loan for Wind Energy GmbH). I also reviewed Hamilton's contract with Kramer. Hamilton had signed the Hamilton/Kramer contract *three weeks prior* to signing the contract with Wachel. This was an important piece of evidence. This showed intent. Von Sauer told me on numerous occasions that they wouldn't have agreed to investing $2 million with Hamilton if he was intending to reinvest the money with Kramer in some far-fetched currency exchange.

I located an email dated June 2015, from Hamilton to Wachel, with a letter attached. In the letter Hamilton told Wachel that the funds were secured in the escrow account. The letter also mentioned that if the escrow account was closed, this would void the funding for the project. This clearly wasn't true. The $2 million was long gone.

I didn't tell Von Sauer this until several months later. The loss of their $2 million and the fact that the contracts Hamilton told them to sign with the various wind turbine companies in Germany, made them defendants in several lawsuits in Germany. The $2 million was just a drop in the bucket compared to what their losses grew to. I felt bad for them, but I have felt bad for all the victims in my cases. Even though my job – which I loved – was to gather and present the facts, I did want justice for the victims in my cases.

I look at the mistakes victims made when being scammed out of millions of dollars. If I put myself in their shoes, without the experience I have had as a white-collar crime FBI agent, would I fall for these same scams? Could I not see the forest for the trees? Would I keep sending good money after bad money? I'm confident if I'd conducted the due diligence needed on Hamilton, I wouldn't have made this deal. In all of my white-collar crime cases there is some type of fraudulent document involved. I use the word "document" in a broad sense. The cliche, "these documents are as good as the paper they're printed on" applies here. As an agent, I have seen, heard and investigated all types of scams. There is always a slightly new twist or two. Hamilton's presentation document is where Von Sauer and Wachel should have conducted their due diligence.

I called Von Sauer (he was residing in Australia with a 15-hour time difference) and broke the news that his money (and Wachel's) was long gone. I could tell he was having a difficult time accepting this. All he had was hope. What else can you have at that point? He kept saying that maybe the money Hamilton sent to Kramer would somehow come through. I explained that I had reviewed the bank accounts and followed the money and assured him the money was gone. There was no escrow account and no currency exchange. I could tell Von Sauer couldn't handle what I was telling him. At that point, Von Sauer put his wife on the phone. I spoke to her for a while and she was very nice. He came back to the phone. Even though he thanked me for the job I was doing, this just made me feel worse for him and Wachel.

Von Sauer and Wachel didn't truly understand our legal system and the FBI. I suspect all he knew about the FBI was the way it was portrayed on television shows and in movies. But I also knew he had an appreciation for what the FBI does and what I was doing. During our conversation, I again explained to him that if and when Hamilton stands in front of the federal Judge, the Judge would order Hamilton to pay restitution. Even though the money was long gone, the judge could require Hamilton to liquidate assets. Hamilton's only income was his military pension and social security. He hadn't generated a dime for almost 20 years. This was an odd piece of evidence, especially since Hamilton was funding or had funded multimillion dollar projects all over the world. I was nervous that Hamilton would scam someone else out of their money and hand it over to Von Sauer and Wachel, like some type of Ponzi scheme.

I began going through Hamilton's WP presentation document. This was the same presentation document Hamilton provided to SA Jasper and I during our initial interview with him. I went through the presentation document page by page. The corporate structure had two names. One listed Hamilton as the president, and the only other officer, a Vice President, had been deceased for several years. The organizational chart featured fictitious names. The 13 locations in the United States and the 19 worldwide locations were also phony. Every one of the completed projects and projects under construction were bogus. The pattern of deceitful information continued throughout the document. Zero plus zero equals zero.

23

WIND TURBINE SCAM: LEVERAGE

The time had come to re-interview Hamilton, almost exactly one year after I had first talked with him. In the first interview I had limited information and facts, which meant limited leverage. This time would be different.

Hamilton had a few choices. He could admit to the fraud and agree to plead guilty or be indicted by a federal grand jury after my testimony. Choices like these allow subjects to have some control of their sentencing. Hamilton had to ask himself, "Do I admit this fraud to the FBI agent so I might receive an offense level reduction for taking responsibility?" Admission would reduce his Federal Sentencing Guidelines offense level. Or would Hamilton turn his back on me and wait for the indictment, which would lead to several agents surrounding his residence early one morning to arrest him. Once indicted, his trial clock would begin ticking. With the advice of his future Attorney he would then decide whether to plead guilty or go to trial. If he went to trial and won, he would walk free. But if he lost, he wouldn't receive any reduced offense levels in the sentencing guidelines. And at that point, I would ask the AUSA to encourage the Judge to consider the top of the sentencing guidelines range. No one wants to go to trial, and besides, "A good agent does not go to trial."

As I prepared for my second interview, I asked SA Jasper to accompany me. By now he was familiar with the allegations and had general knowledge of the case. And I had the leverage to conduct a proper interview.

One area I was prepared to cover with Hamilton was when SA

Jasper and I initially interviewed him. At that time, he told us that 10 years prior he had invested between $2 million and $5 million with Kramer in a currency exchange, and that within about three months he received a return of $75 million. I had an organized list of questions and topics typed up that I wanted to cover in the interview. I felt very confident in my knowledge of the case. I just didn't see how he could possibly convince us that he was innocent.

We again arrived unannounced and knocked on Hamilton's door. He answered and invited us in and we sat in the same den from our previous interview one year earlier. This den had an unusual number of trinkets displayed all over the room. I suspect each one had a story to tell. We could tell that Hamilton's health had diminished since the last time we saw him, and I knew that would play a part in how the case would end. Hamilton's wife was in the house just like before. And once again, she didn't seem interested in being present.

I recall on one occasion, while I was working in the Memphis FBI Division, I was investigating a telemarketing scam. Back in the 1990s telemarketing scams were a popular con. The subject in this case was the manager of a telemarketing company that had scammed hundreds of thousands of dollars from victims all over the United States. It was time for me to attempt a cold call interview of the subject at the subject's residence. As protocol, I had another agent present in the interview. For this interview I had an ace up my sleeve, but I would only use it if the circumstance presented itself. Which it did. The subject had been married for eight years and I had a printout of his criminal history. He had a few speeding tickets, but a few years prior, he was arrested for soliciting a prostitute. This wasn't the sort of thing you'd mention to your wife. I'm sure you see where I'm going with this. And it worked.

When I began asking the subject questions, he kept telling his wife to go to the other room. She refused and a small argument broke out, but he didn't fight it and she was present during the interview. We began with small talk and eventually I moved on to the pointed questions about his direct involvement in the telemarketing fraud. He denied all knowledge about what was going on at the telemarketing company. As usual I was prepared. I had interviewed former employees of the company and I had documents to prove the scam. He remained steadfast in his denial. I changed gears and pulled out a folder and removed his criminal history printout. I didn't show it to him directly, but I held it in the air to review it in front of him and his wife. I said, "It looks like you just have a few speeding tickets. Have you been arrested before?" He said he hadn't. I said, "I see one arrest here. Let's talk about this one…unless I have it wrong.". His wife immediately turned towards him and asked, "An arrest?" I stared at him and smiled. He then stopped the interview and asked to speak to his wife for a few minutes. They stepped away into the kitchen where the other agent and I could watch them for safety reasons. I had my hand on my handgun as it remained in the holster. Did I think something bad would happen? No, but you don't want to let your guard down that one time and get shot up and/or killed. You never know how someone will act when facing criminal charges and prison. I couldn't hear what he was telling her, but he came back to the table and said, "Okay, I will tell you about my involvement in the telemarketing scam."

Later, he pled guilty and received a fairly light sentence. I never knew what he said to his wife that day. Yes, I played the ace to my advantage. Some might call it a "low blow," but what it's really called is leverage.

About three or four years later I was shopping late one night in a Kroger grocery store near my residence. As I walked down one of the aisles a young man was sitting on the floor stocking groceries. Almost at the same time our eyes met, and we acknowledged each other. This was the subject, obviously out of prison and doing what was right; he was working. I was happy to see this. He was very cordial, and we visited for a few minutes and laughed a little about my interview. He told me that as soon as I held up his criminal history printout he knew where the conversation was heading. He thanked me for not saying anything further in front of his wife about his arrest. I didn't ask what he'd said to his wife. I just wished him luck and I continued my shopping.

So as we began interviewing Hamilton, I asked Hamilton to explain his $2 million to $5 million currency exchange investment with Kramer 10 years prior that supposedly netted him $75 million. I was surprised that he continued to go with this story. I gave him an opportunity to tell me otherwise, but at first he held fast. Then I told him he had lied to us about this investment. I asked, "Are you aware that it's a federal crime to lie to an FBI agent? This is a false statement and falls under Title 18 USC §1001." He looked down and said, "Yes, I am familiar with the law. I'm a retired Army Colonel." He then told us that he had not invested with Kramer 10 years prior and his only investment with Kramer was in 2014, using Von Sauer and Wachel's money. Hamilton couldn't explain why he had initially lied to us. Now I had an extra chip in the big game I could play later, if I needed it. I moved on to other areas.

I handed Hamilton a copy of his WP presentation document. Since I had researched this presentation document I was prepared. I told him I knew that the WP Vice President had passed away prior to 2014. Hamilton didn't argue this fact. I went through each foreign location bearing various names and listed as companies under WP's control. Hamilton explained that there were individuals in each of the 19 foreign locations that represented WP, but they never conducted any business for WP nor made any money for WP. There was no physical location. Basically, these were simply individuals Hamilton knew. The 13 United States locations were also representatives of WP, but again never produced any business or did any work for WP.

As I pressed for detail on the WP offices in the United States, Hamilton's answers became ridiculous and sad. I asked about the Portland, Oregon office (listed as lumber operations) and Hamilton stated that a relative owned a lumber broker company in Portland and if any WP projects required lumber, he was all set. Mind you, all of Hamilton's alleged projects were overseas. I asked Hamilton about the WP office in San Francisco (listed as environmental) and Hamilton said that the office was closed and never conducted any business. It gets better. I asked about the WP office in West Texas (listed as a commodity). Hamilton said that this office was a beef business, but the owner was deceased. *I guess when WP builds construction projects overseas, they need to feed the work crews?* I asked about the office in Illinois (listed as a commodity) and Hamilton said that this was a grain business. *Maybe the grain could be used to feed the livestock for the beef business?* I asked questions about a few more locations, but the pattern was the same. These weren't actual WP offices and they produced zero business. Hamilton just felt that if he needed these people in a project he could call on them, so he considered these locations WP offices. This was absurd. Hamilton admitted none of the United States WP offices or the WP foreign offices generated any business for WP.

I moved on to the construction projects listed in the document. It stated that WP was constructing a 300,000 bbl per day oil refinery in Mozambique. Hamilton said that in 2008 he was working with a group in Mozambique, but no construction had been started. Still, he considered this "constructing." I told him that the presentation document was deceiving, since the verbiage clearly stated that WP was constructing the refinery in Mozambique. Hamilton again stated that he considered it constructing since he was working with a group even though there was no plan for construction established. I asked about the statement that WP was contracted to construct hospitals in Ethiopia, Nairobi and Sudan. I asked if these projects had begun and once again he said no. The last item I went over was the statement that WP was working with the US Army Corps of Engineers at bases throughout the United States. Hamilton said that he had submitted a proposal to the Army, but it was turned down. Not one the 20 projects that WP had supposedly completed or were constructing existed. It was all a sham.

I went over the contracts Hamilton had with Von Sauer and Wachel, including the $2 million security deposit Hamilton received and the fact that Von Sauer and Wachel didn't know about Kramer until several months after the funds were transferred to Hamilton. Hamilton admitted that maybe he told Von Sauer and Wachel about the funds being sent to Kramer *after* Hamilton had already sent the funds to Kramer.

Hamilton denied the money was supposed to be held in an escrow account. I showed Hamilton a letter dated June 2015 that stated the funds were secured in an escrow account. This was a very important piece of evidence. I asked Hamilton why he signed a contract with Kramer to invest $2 million with Kramer three weeks prior to signing the $2 million contract with Wachel. He had no answer for this. I had all the leverage in this interview.

I moved on to the Choji funding project in Nigeria. Hamilton required a $1.6 million security deposit to be held in an escrow account with WEC. Hamilton was introduced to the owner of WEC, Linda Koda, by Roper. Roper had been introduced to Hamilton several years prior. Hamilton and Choji signed the $1.6 million escrow contract in 2012. Once Hamilton received the $1.6 million, he promised to provide $150 million in funding after 90 days. Hamilton said that Roper told him he could obtain $30 million towards the $150 million funding through a medium-term note. After a few years this medium-term note would be enhanced to $150 million. Hamilton didn't understand what Roper was talking about but relied on his apparent knowledge. Once the Choji funds arrived in the WEC account, Hamilton needed to email the request to release the funds with an attached signed letter on WP letterhead to Koda. I showed Hamilton several of these letters. Hamilton reviewed them and stated that he didn't authorize nor sign these letters. These were e-signatures and Hamilton claimed the only person who could do this was Roper. As time went on, Hamilton kept waiting for the funding to come through, unaware that the funds were no longer in the escrow account. It seemed that Roper had stolen these funds by utilizing an e-signature with Hamilton name.

After Choji was released from prison in 2017, he traveled to Los Angeles, and this is where things almost literally exploded. Hamilton received a call from Koda explaining that Choji had sent a threatening letter to WEC stating that he was going to blow up WEC if he didn't get his escrow money back. Choji also threatened to kill Hamilton. Almost at that same time, Hamilton received a call from the local police department. They confirmed that Choji had threatened to kill him. Everyone has a breaking point. Hamilton believed Koda told Choji that his escrow funds were gone. Hamilton claimed this is when he learned that the funds had been released. He said he was confused and told Koda that he didn't authorize the release of the funds. Koda told Hamilton that she had the release letters. Also, Hamilton was told he could no longer access the escrow account due to instructions from Roper. Hamilton called Roper and he assured him the funds were still in the account. The funds were in fact gone.

I asked Hamilton why he didn't contact law enforcement when he learned all this. Hamilton didn't have an answer for this. I read off the names of the individuals who received the funds and Hamilton had never heard of them. I conducted a limited investigation trying to track this money, but there were too many rabbit holes to run down. Once again, Hamilton didn't have good answers for my questions. With a few more subject matters covered, the interview concluded. I was satisfied with the results. SA Jasper and I headed back to the Frisco RA.

24

WIND TURBINE SCAM: THE BIG CON

At this point, I believed Roper had conned Hamilton. I began tracking down Roper and located addresses in Miami and Philadelphia. Miami looked like the most promising. I contacted the Miami FBI office and sent a lead requesting an agent to accompany me to attempt a cold call interview of Roper. I traveled to Miami in late November 2018 and met the Miami agent that evening. He picked me up from my hotel and I briefed him on my case as we drove to the address I had for Roper. This agent was new to the FBI, but sharp, with a nice demeanor. I could tell he looked up to me just like I did with the squared-away senior agents when I was a youngster in the Memphis FBI office.

The address was a four-story apartment building. We knocked on the door and after no answer we left but came back a few more times until it got too late in the evening. We agreed to try again in the morning before I flew back to Dallas. We left and had a late dinner at his favorite Cuban restaurant. I have only had Cuban food once before. This food was very good.

Early the next morning, which was a Thursday, the agent picked me up and we tried knocking on the door, but again there was no answer. I was running out of time if I wanted to catch my flight to Dallas, so I did something I preferred not to do unless my hand was forced. I left my business card on the door and we waited in the car for about an hour. Just as we were about to leave for the airport, I received a call from a woman who said she received my card. I told her I was trying to get in touch with Roper. She said that Roper was her father, but he was in Philadelphia and would return this weekend. As usual, I gave her very little information about why I wanted to speak to her father. As we were pulling out of the parking lot, I received a call. It was Roper. I signaled for the agent to stop, and he did as I spoke to Roper.

He was friendly and agreed to meet with me, but he couldn't meet until Monday morning, after he returned from Philadelphia. I told him I would see him Monday morning at his residence in Miami. He agreed. I immediately called my supervisor, SSA Lipton, and explained the situation. Unsurprisingly, he told me to just stay in Miami and enjoy Miami. Three more nights in a hotel plus per diem would probably be more expensive than a return flight back. I told him I would come back and fly out Sunday. Why didn't I stay in Miami even though I was single and knew Miami had a great night life? I have traveled a lot for work and vacationed to some great destinations abroad. It wasn't that big of a deal for me to stay. Besides, it didn't matter much, since the next day, Friday, while I was in the Frisco RA, I received a call from an Attorney in Philadelphia who told me he represented Roper. I couldn't interview Roper without his Attorney. I didn't want to show my hand yet, so I told him I might get back to him. It turned into a short, but humorous conversation. He talked smack about his Philadelphia Eagles and I talked smack about my Dallas Cowboys. This is an important reason why I attempt only cold call interviews.

Now I needed to attempt a cold call interview with Michael Morgan*. Morgan was the individual located in the Los Angeles area who received $1 million from Kramer, immediately after Kramer received the $2 million Von Sauer and Wachel security deposit money from Hamilton. As I mentioned earlier, Morgan had been convicted of a very similar fraud by the Portland FBI office about 20 years prior. I wanted to know what part Morgan played in this charade.

All this can be confusing, but I'll summarize what was known. Von Sauer and Wachel's $2 million was wire transferred to Hamilton, Hamilton immediately wire-transferred the $2 million to Kramer residing in Hong Kong. Kramer then wire transferred $1 million to individuals in China and $1 million to Morgan in Los Angeles. Fletcher received $300,000 from Kramer during this time period. The Choji $1.6 million investment wired to Hamilton from Nigeria appeared to have been stolen by Roper and distributed to five individuals/companies throughout the United States. And then there was the Bulgarian Attorney who alleged Hamilton defrauded him out of millions.

I had a post office box number registered to Morgan at a mail center located in Las Vegas, Nevada. It was late fall 2018, and I was going to be in Las Vegas for a three-day vacation, so I decided to go to the mail center and attempt to obtain information on Morgan. I still had to get approval from SSA Lipton, which was no problem. I think he was impressed, but he joked and asked if I was crazy. (I did this same thing a few years prior in another case looking for information on a subject that had a mail center box in Las Vegas.) I sent a lead to Las Vegas requesting assistance. This was all free for the FBI. It wasn't a big deal for me since I had been to Las Vegas over 60 times and I could afford to burn up a half day of vacation. Hey, I'm a company man. A Las Vegas agent picked me up at my hotel and we headed for the mail center.

This was another young and sharp agent. I guess at that point they were all young compared to my age of 57. Back in the Frisco RA, the younger agents would ask I'd trained to use the Flintlock Pistol while at the academy.

We arrived and walked inside. The mail center was larger than most of the mail centers I had been in. We waited for the customers to clear out and approached a man behind the counter and identified ourselves with our credentials. I asked to see the registration file for a Michael Morgan, who was assigned to a particular mailbox number. He pulled the file and handed it to me and we thumbed through the pages and we found a few addresses in San Clemente, California. I asked the man if Morgan frequented the location because it appeared that he had his mail forwarded to an address in San Clemente. He said he had only seen Morgan once, three years earlier when he opened the mailbox. He told me that Morgan pays an extra fee to have mail forwarded to another address, and explained that within the next two weeks, Morgan was due to renew his contract to keep the mailbox open. I asked him for copies of certain pages in Morgan's registration file. He made the copies and I left him with my FBI business card and asked him to call if or when Morgan renewed his mailbox.

Now I had an address for Morgan in San Clemente, which was the same city where he received the $1 million from Kramer. We left and the Las Vegas agent dropped me off at my hotel and I continued my vacation. Less than a few weeks after I returned to the Frisco RA, I received a call from the man at the mail center and he told me that

Morgan called and paid the renewal fee to keep the mailbox open. I thanked him and I thought my job would be so much easier if more Americans were like him. If Morgan ended up being convicted in this fraud, which was very similar to his 1999 fraud case, he would be looking at a lengthy sentence.

I learned that Morgan was divorced. I had an address in the San Clemente area for Morgan's former wife, Tonya Morgan*, and based on other relevant investigations I conducted, I was confident that she would be willing to assist me in locating Morgan. I also had an address in San Clemente for Morgan's former girlfriend, the woman he was seeing while he was still married to Tonya. I located a court ordered restraining order on Morgan, filed by his former girlfriend. This restraining order had an address for the former girlfriend. If I couldn't locate Morgan, I might attempt a cold call interview with her.

This would be an all or nothing visit. Because if I missed him, it would be highly unlikely that I would have another chance to attempt an interview due to my impending retirement. Even after I retired, I knew that the agent who would be assigned to the case would not pursue Morgan. This would be my last out of town trip for the FBI. I had traveled for the FBI almost 250 times. Most of these trips were flying to the destinations. Over 130 of these trips were for the DOJ Antitrust Dallas office. The other flights mostly included operational travel, undercover work (using my undercover identity), Phase II interviews and training. In contrast, I drove to nearly all my SWAT training locations, due to all my gear.

I contacted the FBI office that covers Orange County, California. An agent from that office was to partner up with me to attempt a cold call interview of Morgan. In mid-July 2019, (45 days before my mandatory retirement) I flew into Orange County. I had a day and a half to try to locate Morgan. I rented a car and checked into my hotel. The agent who would be assisting me lived on the other side of Los Angeles, approximately one and half hours away from San Clemente and was married with children. I didn't want to burn up too much of his time or cause him to have a late night. He had maybe 10 years in the FBI and was motivated and wanted to help. He said that if we needed to work late he would be fine with that.

All these agents I worked with over the years were team oriented and wanted to give 110 percent. Yes, there were a few I wouldn't want to be best buds with. But you hear it, and it is said, within the FBI, we are a big family and take care of each other. My best friend in the FBI, and who is still in the FBI, is SA Erik Tighe. I am 12 years his senior. We call each other brother.

Early the next morning I drove to a designated area to meet this agent and jumped into his car. We headed to the address I had for Morgan's former wife. After making a few passes we set up about three houses from the actual address. The street was busy with cars and people walking up and down the sidewalks. There was always a chance we would be noticed by the residents in the neighborhood and maybe challenged by the local police, not that this has ever happened to me in the past.

We were looking for any activity at this address. We wrote down license plate numbers of vehicles that were parked in front or near the front of the address. The Orange County agent called his FBI office and provided the numbers to be run through the California database. After about thirty minutes, he called his office back and they said they would get to it shortly. I said let me call my office. I called the Frisco FBI office and spoke to the support employee who could run the license plate numbers. She had always been my "go to" person. She was always quick with a response. After we gave each other a hard time, which was the norm between us, she said she would call me back as soon as possible. In less than 10 minutes she called me back with the results. None of the vehicles were registered to Morgan. The agent with me was impressed with my office's quick response.

After several hours, our presence was becoming known. Two guys sitting in a car for hours on a busy street will always be noticeable. Some of the people walked into the street about 20 yards away and began waving at us, and then the camera phones came out. A short time later, I said, "Let's knock on the door." We walked to the door as all eyes were watching us. The home was some type of split-level residence. As we knocked, a guy opened another door slightly and we told him who we were looking for and he said he would call Tonya's son. A short time later, her son came up the stairs with his roommate and we presented our identification. I told him his mother wasn't in trouble but that I needed to speak with her. He gave me her telephone number, but I asked him to call her and hand me the phone, which he did.

Naturally she was surprised. She said she would call back in a few minutes. I gave her my cell phone number. We spoke to the son for a while and he had no problem telling us that his dad was no good. He said his dad never seemed to work, but always had money and yet didn't provide money to him nor his mom. He provided the name of a woman his dad was dating, Julia Maple*. Maple worked as a hostess at a nice hotel in the area. After about 10 minutes, Tonya called me and asked if we could come over to her boyfriend's residence, which was about five minutes away. After she provided the address, we headed to where she was and as we exited the vehicle she came outside and invited us to sit down in an outdoor patio area. We showed her our credentials. I vaguely explained what this was about and told her I was from the Dallas FBI office. I was in town to locate and speak to Morgan. Not to arrest him. At first, I asked general questions about their relationship. She told me that she caught him cheating on her more than once and he treated her badly. She wanted nothing to do with him, so she divorced him. She also explained that he didn't spend much time with their two sons and neither one of the boys were interested in spending time with him.

I asked if she was aware of Morgan receiving $1 million in September 2014. She said she didn't know and never saw any financial changes to their lifestyle. She didn't know of any expensive items he might have purchased. He was frequently on his laptop. He told her he worked with international investments. He was vague about his work. He wouldn't let her look over his shoulder and when she would walk into the room while he was on his laptop, he would shut the lid until she left the room. She didn't trust him. She said he had a safe in the house and that he was the only one who had access to it. She provided the name of the woman he was seeing while she was still married to him. She also provided an address where he said he was living, but she had never been to any of these locations and couldn't confirm that he actually lived there. I asked her if she knew of any other possible location we could find him. She told us that he frequents Bert's Restaurant and Bar* in Dana Point. Dana Point is about 15 minutes north of San Clemente. I thanked her and she said that she would call me if she learned of anything new regarding Morgan.

We had the name of Morgan's former girlfriend, and we located an address for her about 15 minutes away. We knocked on the apartment door and could hear someone inside, but they didn't answer. After knocking again, we waited and still no answer. I left my business card on the door and told the agent we would sit in the car for a few minutes. Maybe if someone was inside they would open the door, see my card and call.

Sure enough the former girlfriend called. I told her I wanted to speak to her about Morgan. She wasn't interested in talking to us. I tried to coax her into meeting with us. I could tell she was very nervous. She still didn't want to speak to us. Another strike out.

I knew my fellow agent was busy preparing for an indictment in one of his own cases and he had spent a very long day chasing shadows with me on my case. I told him that after he dropped me off at my car I was going to go to the Bert's Restaurant and Bar to see if by chance he was there. The agent told me that he could follow me there and we could both go in together. His drive home would bring him past Dana Point, anyway, he said. I again thanked him and said, "Start your long drive to your residence and if by chance Morgan is at the bar, I will call you." This was not an interview you wanted to do alone, not just for safety reasons, but I needed another agent as a second witness. He agreed and he dropped me at my car. I thanked him, and we went our separate ways.

I found Bert's, which was located at the Dana Point harbor, and walked inside. The narrow, small bar area was to the left of the entrance. There were only two women at the bar and they were speaking with the bartender. I walked through the restaurant and didn't see Morgan. I went back to the bar and stood at the opposite end of the bar from where the women were sitting. I think they knew I wasn't there to mingle, since I didn't sit next to them. I waited until the bartender walked over to me. He appeared to be in his 60s. I showed him my credentials and told him who I was looking for and showed him photos of Morgan. I told him I knew Morgan was a frequent customer. The bartender immediately said that he knew Morgan and confirmed that he was a frequent customer. He had been at the bar last week. The bartender thought Morgan was in some type of investment business and Morgan would brag about his success, but other than that the bartender didn't know much about Morgan. Morgan didn't seem to have any particular day or time that he would come to the bar, but it was usually early evening. I left the bartender my card and asked him to call me the next time Morgan showed up. And I asked the bartender to be discreet. The bartender agreed and before I turned to walk away, he thanked me for my service to the country. I felt good about the conversation, until three days later when I received a call from Morgan.

It was a Saturday evening, and I was hosting a pool party at my residence. SSA Lipton was at the party with several other agents. I took the call and went to the other side of my residence. As Morgan began asking the usual questions, I dodged the answers and remained vague. I told him I hadn't come to Los Angeles to arrest him, just to ask him questions about individuals he knew. He agreed to meet with me, though I knew this most likely wouldn't happen. I told him I could meet with him Monday morning in San Clemente and that I would check back with him the next day, Sunday, and we would agree to a time and place.

I spoke to SSA Lipton who of course approved my travel, so I took a few minutes away from the party and began looking at flights. In the meantime, we reached out to the Orange County FBI SSA and told her of the fluid situation and asked if I could have the same agent assist me. But, if not, could another be assigned to assist. This was the same SSA who provided the Orange County agent to assist me on my initial travel to Orange County. Shockingly, she refused and stated that our case wasn't important enough for them to provide assistance. This just doesn't happen in the FBI. The only other time I have heard of an SSA refusing to assist another division with a lead, it didn't end well for that SSA. It has always and should always be, "What can we do for you?" On day one at the FBI academy, one of our class counselors told us, "Your reputation in the FBI begins today." This has a lot of truth to it.

I heard that she requested a one retirement extension, like myself, but she was denied. SSA Lipton was also in disbelief of her actions. I think he wanted to squirt me with a water bottle to calm me down because I was going to call her and light into her with every name in the book times ten. SSA Lipton agreed that this needed to be addressed. I suggested that if she didn't change her attitude that we should get the ASAC involved. I liked him a lot and knew he would make some noise. SSA Lipton said that since things were moving quickly, he would approve another Frisco RA or Dallas agent to travel with me to assist.

The next day, I called Morgan and he didn't answer. I left a message, but he didn't return my call. I texted him a few times, but again he didn't respond. I attempted to force his hand by calling his girlfriend who worked as a hostess at the high-end hotel. She didn't want to speak to me. I tried to explain the situation, including her situation, but she said Morgan told her I wasn't a real FBI agent and to ignore me. Knowing that Morgan had stayed in that hotel with her on occasion, I contacted the hotel manager and had a conversation with him and hotel security. I don't know what happened to her. They might have shown her the door. Morgan stayed under the radar, and I assumed he had left the area.

My retirement hourglass was down to a few grains of sand, and it was time to get this case indicted.

25

WIND TURBINE SCAM: GRAND JURY
INDICTMENT

I began wrapping up my case to prepare for an indictment in the next Grand Jury, which is held once a month in the Eastern District of Texas. Hamilton had hired an attorney, a former United States Attorney, not a former AUSA. United States Attorneys are appointed by the President of the United States for each Judicial District. Which means this United States Attorney was very familiar with FBI investigations. I'm sure this former United States Attorney was expensive.

I need to pause here to share my opinion on this, and I know I share this with other agents. I lose respect for a United States Attorney or AUSA who changes "sides" by leaving the federal prosecutors office to become an attorney hired to defend individuals facing federal prosecution. Of course they do it for the money. They get their experience at the federal prosecutor level and bring that experience to the other side. This means they know the ins and outs of not only how federal cases are run but also the workings of federal investigative agencies such as the FBI. These federal cases need to be prosecuted and the defendants need an attorney, so what is wrong with changing sides? To me it is morally wrong.

The United States Attorney wanted to have a meeting with AUSA Garrett and me. I provided my case summary with the evidence against Hamilton to AUSA Garrett. AUSA Garrett provided a summary of this information to the defense. This is normal and is not the discovery stage. Discovery would be provided to the defense immediately after the indictment. The agent provides all of the government's evidence in the case file to the AUSA and the AUSA provides the relevant evidence to the defense.

They basically wanted to feel us out and see what we had and what our intentions were. Our goal was to convince the defense attorney that it would be in Hamilton's best interest to plead guilty based on our strong case. A guilty plea would naturally save a lot of time and expense on both sides. This would be favorable for Hamilton as far as the charges and the sentencing were concerned, too.

AUSA Garrett and I met the former United States Attorney and another young defense attorney at the United States Attorney's Office in Plano. We provided a summary of our case and what we would charge in an indictment. The young defense attorney made some arguments that were irrelevant and aimless. I almost felt sorry for him, but I think the former United States Attorney let him ramble on just to get the experience of being beaten down by an experienced agent. There always seemed be a medical or personal issue with a subject in my cases offered as an excuse why they couldn't or shouldn't face federal criminal charges. I was expecting this with Hamilton, since I knew he had medical issues and was now into his late 70s. But he was quite capable of using the phone and the computer to scam people all over the world. And this needed to stop.

As expected, they brought up Hamilton's medical issues and claimed that if he was in prison, he wouldn't be able to care for his wife. The year prior his wife appeared healthy. Like my grandmother used to tell me, "The crying room is in the back." They wanted Hamilton to have a mental evaluation to see if he could stand trial. Maybe I'm too aggressive, but I jumped in before AUSA Garrett could respond. I told the two defense attorneys that wouldn't be a problem, but that it also wouldn't affect the indictment. "After the indictment you will have ample opportunity to present the evaluation of Hamilton's mental condition to the Federal Judge," I said. If the doctor's medical evaluation stated that it would be difficult for Hamilton to stand trial, Hamilton would have to authorize the release of the doctor's findings and we could also have him evaluated by an independent doctor. Would this drag the case? Absolutely.

We presented a strong case to the defense, but I didn't want them to drag it on like defense attorneys do. As if the government is going to go away. After the meeting, I told AUSA Garrett that we didn't need to wait on this supposed mental evaluation of Hamilton. We could indict Hamilton and then the defense could still pursue this, but at least we would have the indictment. He agreed. This was a few months prior to my mandatory retirement date. AUSA Garrett was aware that I had requested a year extension to my retirement so I could finish up two cases we were working together. But that date was coming upon us quickly, and it was impossible to stop or delay it. AUSA Garrett was also aware that this was a complex case and I knew my case backwards and forward. He knew, in the long run, that it would be much easier on him if I testified in the Grand Jury for the indictment instead of a new agent. I was two months from the mandatory date, which meant there were only two more dates the Grand Jury was meeting. One of those dates passed and I stressed to AUSA Garrett to indict in August 2019, because the next Grand Jury wasn't until September 2019, after I would have retired. There was another case that AUSA Garrett and I were working on, and I was ready to indict this individual. Our plan was to indict both cases in the same Grand Jury.

We were ready for me to testify in the Grand Jury, which was held in Sherman, Texas. With AUSA Garrett asking me questions in the Grand Jury, both cases were indicted back-to-back, a mere two weeks prior to my mandatory retirement. I was happy the AUSA ran hard with this and helped these indictments come to fruition. I had never tried nor accomplished getting indictments in two cases on the same day, but I was going to go out on top and with a big bang. I felt like I was sprinting across the finish line. (This other case will be discussed in the next chapter.)

Hamilton pled guilty (good agents do not go to trial) and several months later I went to the sentencing and sat in the back. I expected him to enter the courtroom with a walker or a cane looking feeble. The bonus would have been if he wore his Army Colonel duds. He did walk in using a cane and looking feeble. Von Sauer and Wachel were supposed to give a victim statement by video from Germany, but the video connection wasn't working. I was glad that I was just a civilian at that point. I would have been irate at the person responsible for not doing their due diligence prior to the judge entering the courtroom. It was lucky that Von Sauer and Wachel had sent in their victim statements by email or letter. The Judge ordered full restitution, which required Hamilton to sell his residence, a vehicle and make payments through his military pension and social security.

As often as I have traveled Europe by train, especially Germany, I vaguely recall seeing wind turbine farms. I just didn't pay attention. Now when I travel through Europe, I will be more cognizant of these structures being someone's *windfall* or someone's *downfall.* I will reminisce about all the work I put into that case.

During my last year before retirement I had an opportunity to do an undercover assignment on the coast of Florida (I'm being vague on the location, but it would have been nice). I reached out to FBI Headquarters and spoke to one of the persons managing the assignment. I then spoke to SSA Lipton about it and he said I should go for it. After I spent some time thinking about it and weighing my available time, I turned it down, knowing that I might need those two to three weeks. The undercover role sounded like fun, but there is only so much time in a day. Did I miss out on something big? As much as I was involved in, directly and indirectly, while I was an agent, I didn't want to feel as though I left anything on the table. I did want an overseas assignment in one of our Legat offices. At one point I had a "hook" who told me they could get me an assignment. Since it would be my first Legat assignment it would only be six months and not in one of the good locations. But hey, I understood you must prove yourself in a questionable Legat location before they send you to a more desirable location. I just didn't push that button.

I have observed many agents coming down to their last few months before they retire. They were submitting the numerous retirement forms, getting their cases reassigned, shredding documents, packing their desks, turning in equipment and so on, not preparing for two indictments two weeks prior to retirement. I know my SSA was impressed. Right around this time there was an all-office conference, which was watched either in person or via video conferencing by all employees of the Dallas Division, including our numerous RA offices located in various parts of the state. I watched from the Frisco RA as one of our ASACs was excited to announce my accomplishments. He went on and on and I really appreciated his speech and the respect he had for me and my work.

On this day, I was the windshield and not the bug.

26

❦

FINANCIAL RUIN

In 2018, the Frisco RA received a complaint from, Dean Sparks*, alleging that Inman Najera*, defrauded Sparks out of over $500,000 in an investment scam beginning in 2012 and continuing into late 2016. Sparks was retired and this was his retirement money to live on. Without those funds he was ruined financially.

SSA Lipton approached with this complaint and asked me to review it. The main issue was the FBI loss threshold for opening an investigation. $500,000 is a lot of money to lose in a scam, but at the time, the Frisco RA was turning down cases which had a much larger loss amount, due to lack of resources. On the White-Collar Crime Squad, we generally had around seven agents. Our AO covered Collin County and Denton County, Texas, which were two of the top ten fastest growing counties in Texas. We couldn't address all the cases with our lack of resources.

Another factor for me to consider was my mandatory retirement date, which was set for August 2018. I flashed back to 1988, in the first week of the FBI academy, when we were reminded that we had to retire no later than our 57th birthday. I did the quick math and I thought, "Wow, the year would be 2018. So far into the future." I couldn't imagine what 2018 would look like. It seemed like it went in a flash, but when I looked back at the past 31 years as an FBI agent, I realized I covered a lot of ground, which is the very motivation for this book. At the time, I was in the process of submitting a request to FBI Headquarters in Washington DC, for a one-year extension on my retirement date.

The one-year extension request is in a window of six months to three months prior to your actual retirement date. There are steps to take and an official two-page letter that must be submitted. But first you need your SSA's approval, ASAC and SAC approval before this letter is submitted to FBI Headquarters. Once it arrives at FBI Headquarters, I can't tell who pushes the letter through to the FBI Director's desk. But I have seen and heard that some agents don't even get past their SSA's approval, and some are denied when the letter is almost out the door. Obviously, there are a variety of reasons for this.

I knew all three of my superiors were on board for me to submit my letter, but I didn't know how Headquarters would react. Maybe they just flipped a coin. There were strict criteria that you had to address in the letter, or they would just deny your extension. I was surprised and in a bit of disbelief when I learned what FBI Headquarters required. Not only did they not care what you had accomplished as an agent in your career, they didn't want you to cite this in the letter. Instead, they wanted you to cite what you would do for the bureau over the next year that would benefit the bureau. I wrote my two-page letter, and with SSA Lipton's suggestion, I mentioned that I was a recipient of the United States Attorney General's Distinguished Service Award (which is the highest award you can receive as an FBI agent. I'll touch lightly on this later in the book) for my work in the Holy Land Foundation case. After the letter reached FBI headquarters, I received a notification that they were reviewing the letter and would get back to me. A short time later I received the one-year extension, which pushed my retirement date to August 2019.

I reviewed Sparks' complaint and told SSA Lipton that the case didn't seem complex and I could work it as a "fast track" case. Fast track cases shouldn't require a lot of investigative work and the results should be quickly achieved. I said I could open the case and I expect the results before my retirement.

I contacted Sparks and conducted an interview and obtained the information I needed to proceed with my investigation. Sparks was looking for an investment for retirement money so that it would grow into a bigger nest egg. He happened to speak with a former co-worker who was also retired and Sparks told him what he was trying to accomplish. It just so happened that this former co-worker's son-in-law, Najera, was starting up an investment company and might be able to help him. Sparks contacted Najera and Najera told Sparks that he could invest Sparks' $500,000 in a company that invests in currency exchanges. Najera told Sparks that he didn't hold a broker's license but could still invest the money with expected great rates of return. Najera added that he had also invested his in-laws' money. Sparks felt comfortable and trusting of Najera.

In August of 2012, Sparks agreed. But he wanted to test the investment first, so he initially invested $30,000. As expected in these scams, when Sparks received his first emailed (wire fraud Title 18 USC §1343) statement it showed that Sparks' $30,000 investment had increased a substantial amount. As I have seen in numerous investment scams, the subject keeps reeling the victim in for more money.

Once Sparks saw his initial investment increase, he wire-transferred $470,000 to Najera. A short time later, Sparks sent Najera $20,000. Each month Najera emailed Sparks a statement indicating Sparks' investment money was increasing. Sparks was excited to see the dollar figures on these statements increase month after month.

I subpoenaed Najera's bank account records where Sparks' money was deposited by check and wire transfer. As I began reviewing the bank records, the findings were as suspected. The money was not invested but spent by Najera for personal items. I had every detail of these expenditures from $5.30 at Starbucks to $50,000 on a vehicle. There were purchases for airline tickets overseas, airline tickets to and from Dallas and even four tickets to a Dallas Cowboys home game. Also of interest, Najera paid between $5,000 and $30,000 to three in-laws and family members from this account. All funded with Sparks' investment money. With this information, I had an extra leverage chip in the big game. I learned that Najera had a wife and two teenage children. The family would soon be separated with Najera going to Federal Prison.

There were so many small to large expenditures and in the initial bank account where Sparks' funds began, these funds were used to open other accounts in the same bank. I spoke to our forensic accountant assigned to the Frisco RA. He had worked up cases for me in the past with excellent results. I provided him with the bank records and let him do his thing. After a few months, he produced four different spreadsheets, each several pages long. He explained how he produced each spreadsheet and the significance for my case. What I saw is what I had seen in my past cases, but it is still shocking. In less than a year, Najera had spent all of Sparks' investment money on personal items. Sparks' loss was $482,000.

Several months later, Sparks told Najera that he needed $38,000 and told him to withdraw the money from his investment fund. After Najera tried to convince Sparks not to withdraw any funds, Sparks became concerned. Eventually, Najera withdrew the $38,000 and gave it to Sparks. Later, Sparks wanted to close the account and withdraw all of his money, which was now $825,000 (on paper only). Najera kept stalling and giving Sparks excuses about why he couldn't withdraw the money at that time. Najera told Sparks that the money had been embezzled by someone handling the funds where the money was invested. At this point, Sparks knew something was very wrong and he started demanding the money. Najera almost completely stopped responding to Sparks' demands. Sparks learned that Najera moved to a coastal town in Florida.

This is when Sparks contacted our Frisco RA with his complaint. I had Sparks send me Najera's monthly investment statements. There was a statement for each month beginning September 2012 and through December 2016. At the very least, each one of these emailed statements was a separate wire fraud violation. This December 2016 statement indicated that Sparks' investment had grown to $825,000. As I reviewed these statements, I could easily evaluate that these statements were not worth the paper they were printed on. It's far too easy to create statements like these with a bogus investment name and account number. There were a handful of dollar figures showing increases and a few decreases during various points in a month, but each month the investment increased.

Sparks explained that since he had lost all his investment money, he had to sell his country residence, a vehicle, his workshop tools and pieces of furniture and was now living further away in Section 8 housing. He provided me with his new address. At Sparks' age there was no way to start his life over and generate a decent income. I have seen so many victims like Sparks that were on top of the world financially and now were financially ruined. Sparks asked me if he could make a victim statement during Najera's sentencing. Sparks was eager and hopeful that Najera would receive a lengthy prison sentence. I told him that he could make a victim statement when the time came.

I had a criminal history run on Najera, and he had none...except an arrest for embezzling about $5,000 in Florida. This occurred during the time I was investigating this matter. I don't know what the outcome was from this embezzlement, but it didn't matter as you will read later.

I located an address for Najera in a small town near Destin and Fort Walton Beach, Florida. I made contact with the FBI office that covers this territory and arranged for an agent to accompany me in locating and attempting a cold call interview with Najera. In February of 2019, I flew into Fort Walton Beach late in the day and checked into my hotel, which was right on the beach. My room faced the beach, which was approximately 15 yards away, but I never stepped out of my room to walk on the sand. Instead, I stayed in my room and went through the spreadsheets and my notes. I walked to dinner and ate some good seafood and then headed back to my room.

The next morning the local agent picked me up and we drove the 45 minutes to the address I had for Najera. As usual, we set up close to the residence and watched for a while. The residence was small, located in an average neighborhood, but appeared to be well maintained. There was no movement for a few hours, then we saw a vehicle pull into the driveway and the garage door went up, but I couldn't see any of the occupants in the vehicle. It was time for the cold call.

We knocked on the door and a middle-aged woman, Sara Powell*, answered. We identified ourselves and I told her who I was looking for. She said the Najera family had moved out a month ago. Powell invited us in and as we sat down, she told us that Najera, his wife and two children lived with her in her residence for three or four months. As I looked around the cluttered home, I asked, "Did the whole family live here? And why?" She said that she met Najera's wife at their workout facility and Najera's wife mentioned that she and her family needed a temporary place to stay. I asked if she had a forwarding address and she said no but mentioned that they moved somewhere nearby, maybe three or four miles away. Powell told me that almost one month ago, Najera's wife wanted to show Powell their new residence, so Powell followed her there. But Powell couldn't remember the name of the street nor how to find the location.

I thought I was about to strike out on locating Najera. We thanked Powell and as we began walking out the front door, I had a thought and paused. I said, "You mentioned working out with Najera's wife at a gym. What's the name of the gym and where is it located?" Powell told us that Najera's wife was one of the workout instructors at this neighborhood gym. I asked if she knew her schedule or hours. She led us into the kitchen where she turned on her computer and pulled up the gym's website. Her schedule was listed right there. I was either lucky or just living right. Najera's wife was on today's schedule until 5:00 PM. It was just after 3:00. Powell provided us with the address of the workout facility. We thanked her again and walked to our vehicle.

As we sat in the agent's vehicle, we pulled up the address of the gym on Google Maps and I pulled out my folder, which listed vehicles registered to Najera. It was still a long shot, but I had hit many long shots. We located the gym, which was a nondescript building in the middle of a nearby neighborhood. There were 30 to 40 vehicles in the medium-sized parking lot. We found Mrs. Najera's SUV in the second row we passed. I had the agent pull to the back of the parking lot, and back into a parking space so we could watch her SUV, which was now about 50 to 75 yards away. I told the agent, "Let's just sit on the car and see what happens at five." I didn't want to leave, not knowing if Mrs. Najera would leave early. The agent had binoculars, which any good agent should keep in their vehicle. The agent asked what I wanted to do when Mrs. Najera came out of the facility. At this point, I was making decisions on the fly. I have had to do this in other similar situations. On SWAT, our initial plan to effect an arrest is rehearsed several times but can change in a flash once the team leader says, "Execute."

I wanted to see if I was really living right. I was counting on her simply driving to their residence while we followed her. Of course, I also hoped Najera was at the residence so I could at least have the chance to interview him.

If we simply walked up to Mrs. Najera, identified ourselves and asked her about her husband, she would have too many options to defeat my plan of a cold call interview of her husband. She could call him while we were talking to her, tell us he was out of town, tell us she wasn't going home any time soon then call him from her SUV. None of those options were good for me.

At 5:10 PM, Mrs. Najera had not exited the facility. I was becoming a little concerned, but 5 minutes later she walked out and as she was entering her SUV, I told the agent to move slowly and fall in behind her at a distance. She turned left and we stayed about 20 yards behind her. She was driving through the neighborhood making a turn here and there, and we were clueless about where she was heading. After she made three or four turns, she might have noticed the same vehicle was still behind her. I hoped she wasn't paying attention and instead, was distracted on her cellphone. Since we were staying about 30 to 40 yards behind her I was concerned that she might drive up to a busy intersection and we could lose her. Sure enough, she made a right turn onto a busy road and drove through the green light into another neighborhood. We got stuck in traffic, but the agent did a great job getting us through the light. Now we were over 100 yards behind her. Hopefully I didn't bark too loud, but I told the agent to speed up. The agent took off, and Mrs. Najera turned left down one of the streets. As we came upon the street that we thought she turned down, we turned and the agent sped up again and sure enough, there was Mrs. Najera's SUV. We closed fast. She turned right and pulled into a driveway and parked behind a pickup truck. I told the agent not to park on the street, but to pull into the driveway and block Mrs. Najera's SUV. As we stopped close behind the SUV I was already out of the vehicle.

I pulled out my credentials and quickly moved to the driver's side of the SUV. Just as I had thought, Mrs. Najera was talking on her cell phone. I approached the SUV and showed my credentials through the window. Mrs. Najera exited her SUV. I told her I wanted to speak with her husband who I knew was inside (I didn't actually know, but presumed the pickup was his). My bluff worked. We followed her into the house and there was Najera sitting at the kitchen table looking at some paperwork.

We identified ourselves and, as expected, he was shocked. I told him I was from the Dallas FBI office and was here to speak to him about Sparks' investment money. They had two very large dogs in the house, which didn't bother me since I'm a huge dog lover. I followed him, and the other agent stayed in the kitchen, while he put the dogs in the backyard. When we returned, Mrs. Najera was in the kitchen and Najera's two teenage children had just walked into the kitchen from the back of the house. This wasn't optimal, but he did the right thing and told his wife to take the kids in the SUV for a drive. The other agent moved our vehicle from the driveway so she could leave with the children.

We all three sat at the kitchen table for some small talk and I asked him about Sparks' investment money. I think he assumed I had just opened the case yesterday and knew very little. He told me that they were renting this residence and as we walked in, he was searching online for a job. I let him ramble on, telling me that the money was going to be invested in a workout facility that he and his wife would operate, but that it was currently tied up in another company that was handling the investment. I asked him about his family members and in-laws receiving money from this account and he said that he was paying back loans he had with them. I told him that he told Sparks that they had invested their money with him. He didn't reply to my statement. I really didn't want him to go on and on telling me lies, so I stopped him and opened my folder and pulled out the spreadsheets. I handed one to him and told him that the information in the spreadsheet is from the bank accounts he opened with Sparks' investment money. I told him to look through the information. He began turning pages and would occasionally pause to stare at the entries. He stopped after several pages and sat back in his seat. I told him he was facing numerous counts of wire fraud.

I explained that he had two options. He could cooperate right here and now, by admitting to what he actually did with Sparks' investment money. This would mean that he would plead guilty to an information and avoid indictment. If he chose this option, I would make it known to the AUSA of his full cooperation and this would reduce any time he was facing. Or option two, he could be indicted at the next Federal Grand Jury, which was within the next month. I explained that one early morning after the indictment, his residence would be surrounded by FBI agents wearing raid jackets. They would pull him out of his residence and place him under arrest. I told him I hoped his children wouldn't be here to witness his arrest. I wasn't being cold, nor was I bluffing, this is what would happen.

I pointed to the spreadsheet that listed his family members and in-laws receiving money from this account and told him I would be interviewing them to determine what their involvement was in this scam. Then I told him that there is no way his wife thought that they had $500,000 to spend in one year, so I wondered what her involvement was. Option two really upset him and he admitted he didn't want any of that to happen. I reminded him that those were his only two choices.

He sat back in his chair again. I'm sure a lot was going through his mind. I went on to explain that if he decided not to cooperate after his indictment, the case would head to trial and he could take his chance in front of a jury. But Sparks would testify and the jury would learn that this elderly man was financially wiped out and living in Section 8 housing because of Najera. I'm sure Najera was thinking to himself, *What just happened? One moment I'm sitting comfortably at my kitchen table then the next moment there are two FBI agents in my kitchen changing my life.*

He struggled to figure out what he wanted to do. He asked if he should get an attorney. I told him straight up that I couldn't give him that advice. I simply stated that if that's what he decided to do, we would get up now and leave, which meant he chose option two. He leaned in and started looking at the spreadsheets again, stopped, and said, "I don't know what to do here."

As we waited and waited, I picked up the spreadsheets, placed them in my folder, and closed my notebook. I stood, and the other agent followed my lead, then I said, "We will leave now. I'll see you soon." He stopped us before we could take a step toward the door. He asked us to sit back down and then admitted to everything. He cried. This was not my first nor my second subject to cry. I calmed him down and he appeared to stop crying. When he finished, I told him I had no need to talk to his wife, which at that moment I thought was true. He then mentioned suicide, and the other agent and I began to work more diligently to calm him. I told him that he had a great wife and two teenagers to raise. I told him that this would all be behind him someday and then he could go forward with his life. Understandably, these situations are incredibly stressful. Eventually, he calmed down.

This wasn't the first time one of my subjects had mentioned suicide. One mentioned suicide to someone the night after I had interviewed him, and he had admitted to the fraud. I received a phone call telling me that the police picked him up and took him to a facility that watches and evaluates people who mention suicide. He was released the next day. Before his sentencing date, his wife left him and took the two children. At his sentencing, while I was waiting for the judge to enter the courtroom, she came up to me and introduced me to a man she was now seeing. Bring a date to your almost ex-husband's sentencing? Who does this?

The other person was my main subject—the only female subject I had ever had in my career. I was working in the Memphis FBI Division in the mid 1990s. This case involved a small printing company that was forced to close its doors because a long-time employee, my subject, had embezzled funds. The printing company had been in the same family since they opened in the 1920s. The employee was a woman who had worked for the company for many years. She was the only person who worked in the accounting department. She handled accounts receivables, accounts payables and payroll. She was paid a weekly salary. She wrote and signed her own paychecks like she had done for years. Then she began writing herself two checks per week, then three, then four, then five. She embezzled more than $800,000 in over three years.

When I interviewed the owner, he couldn't figure out why they were no longer profitable, but never thought that his long-time employee was stealing from the company. He was very naive. Why was this a federal violation? The company was in Memphis, and she lived and banked just across the Tennessee border in Mississippi. Memphis is nuzzled right next to Mississippi to the south and Arkansas to the west. This was in violation of Title 18 USC § 2314, interstate transportation of stolen money/securities. In other words, she crossed the Tennessee border into Mississippi with the stolen money. I interviewed employees at the Mississippi bank and told them that their long-time client had deposited one paycheck a week for years, and now she was depositing five every week. Didn't they notice something? They hadn't, though in today's world the bank would likely have reacted differently.

When she learned I was investigating her, she committed suicide. At first, I wasn't sure I believed this. Maybe the information was false. Did she leave the country? I confirmed the death through a death certificate. I ended up going after her husband, because most of the stolen money was being used in his small auto repair business. At first, he denied this, until I showed him all of his personal expenditures, which far exceeded his auto repair business revenue. After pleading guilty, he went to federal prison.

As we finished up, I explained the legal process and that to avoid the indictment there would be a plea agreement and at that time he would be required to have an attorney. As we were about to leave, I asked him to call his wife. He did and I took the phone from him and walked away. I asked if she was close by and she said she was on the street. I told her we were leaving and we would wait for her to pull into the driveway. I explained that her husband was depressed and had mentioned suicide, so I asked her to keep an eye on him and that he would explain this matter to her.

A short time later, after I was back at the Frisco RA, AUSA Garrett contacted me and told me that he received a call from an attorney who is representing Najera, but Najera had not paid him yet. Najera had indicated that he wanted to plead guilty and avoid the indictment. I'm sure AUSA Garrett was ready to turn over our evidence to this attorney so that he could review and make sure Najera was making a sound judgement. After a few months or so without any progress, I called AUSA Garrett and asked if he had spoken with Najera's attorney. He said no. Garrett then called the attorney and after a lengthy phone tag, the attorney explained that he still had not been paid and he was going to give Najera one more chance before he dropped him as a client. Since Najera was technically represented, I couldn't contact him. Later, the attorney contacted AUSA Garrett and told him he had dropped Najera. AUSA Garrett asked if Najera had hired another attorney and he said he didn't know. Within a day or so the same attorney contacted AUSA Garrett and said Najera planned to pay him. We were now four or five months removed from February, when I interviewed Najera. As mentioned in a previous chapter, there were only two Grand Jury dates available before I retired. A short time later, again, the attorney called AUSA Garrett and informed him that, due to nonpayment, he longer represented Najera. I immediately called the attorney and he confirmed that Najera kept telling him he would pay him but never did.

We were now past the July Grand Jury date. I told AUSA Garrett we needed to get this indictment in August along with the Hamilton case. He agreed, knowing this was my last shot at it.

The day before the Grand Jury, I contacted Najera and told him that he would be indicted tomorrow in the Grand Jury held in the Eastern District of Texas in Sherman, Texas. He was taken aback by this. I told him he had dragged this out too long, but I would make a deal with him. I told him I wouldn't send agents to his residence and have him arrested if he promised that he would travel from Florida to Sherman, Texas to turn himself in to the United States Marshal's office the day after tomorrow's indictment. I'm not easy but I can be had. I told him I would meet him at the Marshal's office. He agreed and I warned him not to dismiss this. He was apologetic and said he would be there, and he was.

The next day, approximately two weeks before I was no longer going to be an FBI agent, I testified in the Grand Jury in both cases, back-to-back. After my testimony, the standard practice is for the

AUSA to ask the Grand Jurors if they have any questions. From time to time I might get one or two questions, but generally not. The Grand Jurors said no. So as is the norm, the AUSA Garrett told me to step out of the Grand Jury room while they voted on a "True Bill" (indictment) or a "No Bill" (no indictment). The "True Bill" basically means that there is enough evidence in the case to show that a crime has been committed and the matter would go to trial, unless there is a plea agreement before the case reaches trial. In a Federal Grand Jury indictment setting there is no judge or defense attorney present. Just the AUSA and, in my case, myself and the Grand Jurors. In trial, you need a unanimous vote by the jury for a conviction. But on the other hand, it is more difficult to get a Grand Jury indictment versus a Congressional Impeachment of a United States President.

As I waited outside the Grand Jury room, I looked down at my suit, thinking, *It will be a long time before I'm wearing this sharp suit again,* AUSA Garrett came out and said we need you back in the Grand Jury. I was surprised. What questions could they possibly have? What did they miss? I was sure my testimony hit it out of the park. I walked back into the Grand Jury room with AUSA Garrett leading the way. AUSA Garrett told the Grand Jurors that this was off the record. He mentioned that I would be retiring in two weeks with the FBI's mandatory retirement. AUSA Garrett went further and said I was an excellent agent and would be missed in the FBI and the United States Attorney's office. A loud ovation followed, and I was in awe. To receive these comments and respect from AUSA Garrett made me feel like an accomplished FBI agent. Later, at my retirement party, AUSA Garrett made a longer speech on my behalf.

Several months later, Najera was sentenced by the Federal Judge. I had believed Najera was looking at a three-to-four-year sentence in federal prison. But I had not reviewed the Federal Sentencing Guidelines in this case. Sparks made his victim statement before the Judge and the Judge imposed an "upward departure," sentencing Najera to 10 years in federal prison. I was surprised. This has happened only once or twice in my other cases. You mostly hear about a judge imposing a "downward departure" on the suggested sentencing guidelines.

I heard Najera appealed his sentence later, but the appeal was denied by the Fifth Circuit of Appeals.

27

⌐•⌐

UNDERCOVER WORK

There are undercover roles I can't write about have been left out of the book, but I will discuss a few in as much detail as allowed.

I was undercover certified after successfully completing an undercover school in 1992. My greatest memory from the school came after a few days of class. The instructor was standing in front of the class when he announced that a special guest was there to speak to us. Stepping out of the darkness, there he was, none other than the greatest, or one of the greatest, FBI undercover agents of all time: Joe Pistone aka Donnie Brasco. The whole class just stared in awe. I had read Pistone's 1988 book *Donnie Brasco* and later watched the 1997 movie of the same name. Pistone was a pioneer in long-term FBI undercover work. When he began to speak, I immediately thought, *This was an FBI agent? What kind of FBI agent speaks the way he does?* His voice was rough, and he cursed a lot. Then I thought, *Now I see why he was so successful infiltrating the Mafia Bonanno Family.* His undercover work scored over 100 Mafia members' convictions. He pushed the absolute outer edges of the undercover envelope. He had that rough, tough and in-your-face style. This was something I didn't have, nor would I ever have. If I tried, I would be sleeping with the fishes on the very first day. He spoke to us for a while, gave us some tips, told some stories and was to the point on everything he said to the class. He was clearly someone you would love to have a beer with.

This is the thought process for how I determined if I would step out on a limb and act in an undercover role. First, I would only accept an undercover role that involves more or less a white-collar crime role.

I couldn't do undercover work in drug cases, gang related cases or other similar types of violations. Honestly, you could put a pile of cocaine and a pile of flour in front me and I probably couldn't tell the difference. I also wouldn't accept an undercover role in a city where I was assigned. Memphis for one, and especially not in Dallas, since I grew up in Dallas. Too many potential complications. I'm sure my thought process was in line with other agents who considered undercover roles.

Second, when presented with a particular undercover role, I asked myself two questions. Do I have an interest in the undercover role and, can I do the undercover role? There were very few that I recall where I could do the undercover role but didn't want the role. While I was in the Memphis division, another agent, who I knew and worked out of another FBI office, called me and said he had a great undercover role for me. Don't get too excited here, because I turned it down for good reasons. The role was to manage a strip club. There were various types of illegal activity going on in the club, including money laundering.

I knew I could play that role and I'm sure I would enjoy it, but the negatives outweighed the positives. For example, what if dancers wanted a certain day off or maybe better hours and came on to me to get what they wanted? Or maybe they just wanted to fool around. How would I turn them down without arousing suspicion towards me? Tell them that I have a girlfriend or a wife? That wouldn't fly. For argument's sake, what if I accepted their offers, how would I explain that if I had to testify in federal court? Or, if I did turn it down and the defense called dancers to the stand and they lied in their testimony and said that we did fool around, how would I deal with that? I had no interest in jeopardizing my career as an FBI agent. This role was not for me.

Another role I turned down was located in Las Vegas, even though I thought I would be successful in the role and knew I would have enjoyed it. My role was to be a wealthy money launderer working with an FBI source, who would be in a group fixing sporting events. I would have worn expensive clothes, had an expensive sports car and resided in a Las Vegas condo close to the Las Vegas Strip. I already had the Lombardo clothes for the role, and the condo was in place. I just lacked the car. The role required travel all over the country. This sounded right up my alley.

When I was considering the role, I flew to an undisclosed location and met with the case agent and was introduced to the source, who had been in prison for half of his life for murder. The source had very recently been released from prison. After the case agent was impressed with me, he left me alone with the source in a hotel room to see if we could develop a working relationship. As expected, we were opposites, but could we work together to make this undercover case a success? I was the dirty, wealthy businessman and he was the rough and tough guy just released from prison. He was unpolished and all he wanted to do was party, raise hell and chase women. The case agent made it clear to me that my role also included keeping the source under control. I needed to basically watch everything he did 24 hours a day. This could pose a huge risk and lead to numerous problems. After spending a few hours with him, I realized this was beyond what I wanted to undertake. I could handle the actual undercover role, but the additional work to control the source was another matter. I turned the role down and later heard from another undercover agent that the case ended up being very problematic. Maybe I dodged a big hornet's nest.

When I arrived in the Dallas division, I immediately placed my name on a list to transfer to the Frisco RA (at the time it was the Plano RA, but the office moved to Frisco). This was a highly sought-after office. My name was placed on a list for the transfer, but I had no hook. After a ten year wait, my name finally came up. The only reason my name came up was I now had a hook. I'll touch on this later, but I was one of the case agents in the Holy Land Foundation terrorism case, which led to being awarded the highest award you can receive as an FBI agent, the United States Attorney General's Distinguished Service award. My hook paid off. And I was very happy with my assignment to the Frisco RA. When agents asked me what my commute time from my residence to the office was, I said, "About two or three songs long."

While in the Frisco RA, sitting at my desk, I read an FBI communication seeking a qualified certified undercover agent for a role in Miami. The communication had a long list of what qualified the agent for this role—the case agent will list the skills the undercover agent must possess plus the age range, race and gender, etc. I had all the skills listed. The closing date was in three weeks to submit your name and qualifications. After I read the communication several times, I knew I fit the undercover role perfectly and would have enjoyed the role. The role was for a rich money launderer who had a place on the water, an expensive car and frequently traveled to various Caribbean Islands. A no brainer for me. Or was it? I read the communication and thought long and hard but kept pushing it away.

A few days later, I reread it and thought about it again. The reason I didn't put in for the role was the fine print in the FBI communication. The communication said that the undercover role could last up to two years (which was okay with me) and at the conclusion of the role, you would be sent back to your office, which in my case Dallas (I was very happy with that). But the fine print also stated that if you are located in an FBI Division RA, "We could not guarantee that you would return to your Division's RA." This was the decision of your division's upper management (SAC and or ASAC). This was the killer for me. I had waited ten years to transfer to the Frisco RA and if the Miami undercover role lasted six months, a year or two years I could very well end up back in the Dallas office. I wanted the Frisco RA guarantee. So I slid the communication under a pile of papers and let the date expire. Maybe I was the bug and not the windshield in this decision. I don't know if I made the right decision.

I only put in for one undercover role that I didn't get and that was a role that would have put me in China. It was an odd undercover role, and I won't go into the details, but it wasn't spying, it was working with Chinese law enforcement.

28

ONE DAY, ONE HOME RUN

There are white-collar crime undercover roles that can be successfully completed, by design, in a one-day operation. In the summer of 1997, I received a call from an agent in Missouri* asking if I would be interested in a one-day undercover operation there. The case agent said that FBI Headquarters had provided my name as a certified undercover agent with a skillset in gambling operations who could operate a roulette gambling table. He explained that this investigation was an Interstate Transportation in Aid of Racketeering case, also known as ITAR case. And the case involved public corruption of elected officials on the state level. The case agent asked me if I was interested. The answer to both questions I would ask myself was yes. I have the skill to do this role and I have the desire.

The illegal gambling operations, dubbed "Casino Nights", had operated in the past. I would be working with and for a cooperating witness (working with the FBI as a source) who would introduce me to some of the subjects of the investigation. My background for this operation was that I was from out of town but staying in the area with my girlfriend. Also, I was a former dealer who worked in Las Vegas and experienced with operating numerous blackjack and roulette tables. This casino night operated out of a pricey country club located in a rural area. There would be three blackjack tables and one roulette table. The one roulette table would be my role. But if needed, I was skilled in the operation of a blackjack table. One of the blackjack tables was operated by the cooperating witness and the other two blackjack tables would be operated by individuals who were not a party to the

180

undercover operation. The tables and gambling chips were provided by the cooperating witness. They expected between 100 and 150 patrons, which included friends of the state officials and some traveling to the country club from other states.

I knew every payout of the roulette table and there are many. For example, if you put your chip on one particular number and the ball lands on your number it pays 35 to 1. Not only did I know and understand the payouts, but I could also calculate these payouts quickly in my mind. While growing up, my math skills always well exceeded my classmates. I also knew the rules and the hand motions of the roulette dealer. I always said that gambling on the roulette table was the "drunks' game" because it required no skill. You could be drunk and it didn't matter.

The only thing I was lacking, which I thought would be a snap to learn, no puns intended, was the snap of the ball (pill) as you placed it in a rolling motion on the roulette wheel. I needed to train for this. The Memphis FBI office had a contact at one of the casinos in Tunica, Mississippi. It is standard that FBI offices have contacts at casinos. Tunica is located about 45 minutes south of Memphis. After my training was scheduled, I traveled to the casino and met with security and the casino employee in charge of training the gambling table employees. The casino wasn't apprised of the purpose of training. I assumed they could guess that it was for some type of FBI undercover operation.

I went upstairs to the casino training room where they had several blackjack, craps and roulette tables. The training staff member and I were the only two in the training room. I was told that I would have two hours of training, which mostly consisted of practicing the snap of the roulette ball, which places it in motion on the roulette wheel. I asked her how long the regular training was for the roulette wheel. She told me one to two weeks. I told her that it should be easy for me to learn to snap the roulette ball. She said that it looks easy, but if you don't snap it correctly your wrist will soon hurt. She showed me the motion and at first it wasn't easy. In the beginning, my wrist was a little sore. But after some practice, I felt comfortable and after two hours I left with a better education on the operation of the roulette table.

I flew into Missouri and the case agent picked me up at the airport and briefed me on the case. We arrived at the hotel I would be staying in, and I was disappointed with myself because I didn't have my game face on. In any undercover role your mind should be totally focused on who you were pretending to be. I walked up to the hotel front desk to check in. As in a normal undercover role, my reservation was in my undercover name. When the lady behind the registration desk pushed the paperwork in front of me to sign in the hotel, I was still in a conversation with the case agent. I signed the hotel registration paperwork with my real name. As I was pushing the signed hotel paperwork back to her, I immediately woke up and pulled it back and resigned the registration using my undercover name, over my real name. The signature just looked like a scribbled doctor's signature. She didn't notice, but I didn't want to make a mistake like that in a more important setting.

As anyone can imagine, undercover work is basically acting. The difference is, when an actor or actress makes a mistake and says the wrong line you hear "cut" and they do it again and maybe several more times until they get the line right. In an undercover role, if you make that mistake you won't hear the word cut, you may literally get cut by the subject or ruin the case.

This is why it's so important to have your game face on once the undercover role begins. Can it be a little scary? Yes, but you volunteered and trained for this. Oh, and by the way, there is no extra pay for doing undercover work. I don't recall being scared or nervous even when I was on a SWAT team arrest and we were lined up at the door waiting to hear, "Execute, execute." I look back at these undercover roles or SWAT team arrests and wonder to myself, *What were you thinking David, why the extra risk?* Then again, today, I have no interest in riding a 100-mph roller coaster even though I loved it in my earlier years.

The next day began with briefings from the case agents and I met the cooperating witness. I knew and expected the difficulties of operating the roulette table compared to operating a legitimate roulette table in a Las Vegas casino. I didn't have a pit boss, nor cameras, which could back up or correct any actions and there was no security if any of the patrons became belligerent with me. I was on an island here and just needed to take control and be on my toes. The casino operation would begin at 7:00 PM and end at midnight. I dressed in casual clothes and had no weapon.

Now it was game on. At approximately 5:30 PM, the cooperating witness and I arrived at the country club parking lot and began unloading the tables. I was introduced to a couple of the subjects and they looked me up and down and thanked me for being there. I knew I was in. My two cover agents remained in their vehicles in the country club parking lot. There were several very large windows, which would allow the cover agents to observe me standing behind my roulette table. If for some reason things went south, the cover agents could react and take care of business. This comfort level quickly changed. As I was setting up my table, gambling chips and testing the ball on the roulette table wheel, several country club employees closed the blinds and began using white paper and tape to cover all the windows. My island just became smaller but I held firm. The Missouri FBI office and agents assigned to this operation were depending on my success. I continued my practice of correctly snapping the roulette ball and organized my chips.

Patrons began flowing in and the gaming area was crowded and loud. Most were nicely dressed for the occasion; men in their slacks and some wearing jackets and ties, women in cocktail dresses. There was plenty of food and drinks at various tables throughout the country club. My table was always crowded with gamblers hooting and hollering, all in a festive mood. A lot of money was being gambled on my table. These weren't 25 cent chips. These patrons had money.

The table was running smoothly, except on a few occasions when patrons made bets after I motioned by sliding my hand above the table indicating no more bets. Maybe they had never played roulette. Once I snapped the ball and put it in play, I waited for bets to hit the table, but well before the ball began its descent onto the wheel, I extended my arm out and motioned my hand across the table meaning no more bets. On a few occasions, patrons would bet after my hand motion. I had to explain to them that they couldn't place a bet after I motioned across the table. Even though most of the patrons were loud and a little rowdy at my table, they followed the rules after I sternly warned them. What was I going to do, call the pit boss or security? I received a lot of tips in cash and chips. Once midnight arrived, we began shutting down and one of the subjects told me that I did a good job and paid me my fee of $50 in cash. My tips and my pay were turned in to be placed in evidence for the case.

The next day I flew back to Memphis and approximately three months later I received a note from the case agent. He told me that the subjects were indicted. I was later told that when the subjects learned that there was an undercover FBI agent operating one of the gambling tables, they pled guilty. In a nice handwritten note, he thanked me for the excellent work I did. A home run and job well done.

29

<hr />

BRIEFCASES FULL OF CASH

The only time I had an issue with my SSA in the FBI happened while contemplating a possible undercover role in 1999. I had recently arrived in the Dallas division and was assigned to one of the white-collar crime squads. I had been given very little case work. I was mostly assisting other agents with their case work. I was contacted by a Miami* agent who was the case agent on a money laundering investigation. The subjects were two Middle Eastern men who operated a large financial institution in Miami, and they were laundering large amounts of cash from an illegal enterprise through their business. The case agent was looking for a Middle Eastern male who was certified undercover.

The Miami agent told me that according to FBI Headquarters I fit the profile for this undercover role, and he wanted to know if I was interested. He provided me with the case summary. I was interested and asked him to send me the more detailed packet so I could read through the information and decide. When I received this thick packet, I spent some time reading through it and I thought I would and could handle this role. Almost that same day my SSA called me into his office and asked about this Miami undercover role and why I hadn't said anything to him about it yet. I told him I first wanted to read the packet to determine if the role was for me. I told him I had just finished reading the packet and that I was going to put in for the role. He immediately told me I had too much work here on the squad and he wouldn't approve it. He continued reading something on his desk as he said this to me. I shot back and told him that I was still going to put in for the role. He dropped his pencil and looked up at me and said, "You don't understand. I will not approve this." I responded, "Regardless I will be putting my name in for the role." I left his office thinking he was interfering with my career goals. He should have been encouraging me like any good SSA would do.

The next morning I was waiting for the elevator at the Dallas FBI office. When the doors opened, I stepped in and the SAC of the Dallas Division was on the elevator. Was my tie straight? He smiled at me and said, "Good luck in Miami—make the Dallas Division proud." The door opened and he stepped out of the elevator. That is how I knew I had the undercover role. My SSA said nothing to me.

In the undercover role in Miami, I would be depositing money from my "illegal gambling operation" into this financial institution. Once I told the subjects what I was doing and they knowingly accepted the illegal cash, they were laundering the money.

I flew to Miami and met with the case agents and we discussed the particulars. We met in a hotel room. This wasn't the same hotel I would be staying in. I had to play the role as if I was wealthy and stayed in the nicest hotel and drove an expensive vehicle, which I rented each time I arrived in Miami. My hotel room was a penthouse suite at the Luxury Hotel* located right on the beach in Miami overlooking a harbor filled with yachts. The hotel had two penthouse room floors. These were very expensive rooms. Only a penthouse guest had access to a hospitality room. The hospitality room had remarkably unique food and any type of drink you could desire, all free and the staff waited on you hand and foot. This wasn't something I was accustomed to. Some evenings I hung out in this setting with the rich and watched them drink their brandy, cognac and read the Wall Street Journal while sampling the exotic foods. I played the part well, socializing and acting as though I was first class and not steerage.

I was introduced to the subject by an FBI source and soon afterward I opened an account at the financial institution with a large amount of cash. I was always wearing the ol' Nagra body recorder. The Nagra recording device was popular and one of the most advanced of its time. It was approximately 4 inches by 3 inches by 1 inch. The device had a pinhole switch to turn the device on and off. The problem was when you turned the device on with the wired remote you didn't necessarily know that it was on unless you could look directly into a pinhole to see the flashing low profile green light. I always checked it before I was on scene. Bathrooms were good spots for this. It's not like you could look at it when it was taped to you. Or you could attach one or two thin wires for the microphone and another wire for the remote on and off switch. I used both, so I had to deal with the wires. Sometimes I would cut a pinhole in my shirt or pants for the wired microphone. I don't recall ever having a problem; the recording was remarkably clear back then. Once I turned the device on I couldn't turn it off until the meeting with the subject(s) was concluded. If you turned the device on and off during any undercover assignment, a defense attorney would have a field day with you on the stand. The device stayed on, even while I was standing at the urinal. Just part of the job. The case agent would place the device on me while we prepped in the second hotel used for the meeting with the case agents. I think back and wonder how any of us wore that device. But back then that was the technology.

I traveled to Miami on several occasions to deposit cash in the financial institution and mingle with the subjects so they could notice me making the deposits. I learned that I was the only one who had signature authority on the account, which of course was established with my undercover identity. I suggested to the case agents that there should be another undercover agent who had signature authority on the account, in case something was to happen to me. He agreed and another undercover agent's name was added to the account, which came in handy later.

After each meeting at the hotel, I was given between $50,000 and $200,000, all in $100 bill denominates, to deposit in this financial institution. The cash was placed in a solid briefcase. When I walked several blocks in downtown Miami to the financial institution, I wasn't too nervous because I had two cover agents. One walked parallel with me, across the street, and one tailed me. I was never armed when I was in an undercover capacity. I didn't feel the need and I didn't want questions from the subject(s) if it became known. Each time I walked into the financial institution the attractive secretary would take me to the count room. She would place the $100 bills in the bill counter. I flirted with her in order to obtain as much information about their operation. Was she aware of the money laundering? Their fees?

One day I received an invitation from one of the subjects to attend a formal party they were giving for clients and others. This seemed like a great opportunity to get the subjects one on one and discuss business.

I informed the case agents and they immediately said I should bring a date to the party. There was only one undercover female agent available for that evening. I told the case agents that we didn't look like we belonged together. They agreed. They said I should ask the secretary at the financial institution to go to the party, which had several obvious advantages. However, there was also one negative: I would be recording and since I wasn't working with another undercover agent, my "date" might say something inappropriate to me during the investigation. Not that I saw myself as being enticing, well okay maybe. I didn't expect her to say anything sexual, but I figured if by slim chance it happened, I could deflect it. Part of my training was that I had to be quick on my feet.

I went into the financial institution to deposit more cash and in the count room I asked if she was going to the party, and she said yes. I told her I received an invitation and she explained that only the more distinguished customers received these invitations. I thought, *Well of course I fit into this category*. I asked her to go with me. She hesitated and said that maybe she shouldn't go out with a client. With my best flirt, I jokingly said, "But I don't have a problem going out with you." She bounced back and said, "Okay, but I'll just meet you at the party."

So I dressed in my expensive Lombardo's suit, drove my Porsche 911 (rented under my undercover name. What can I say? These look and act rich undercover roles do have benefits), valet parked and met her at the party, which was held at a really nice venue. We hung out, walked around, spoke to people and thankfully she didn't say anything inappropriate. Unfortunately, the subjects were always with family members at the party. I didn't observe the subjects speak to any of the other attendees without a family member present. By their mannerisms, they didn't seem interested in talking business. Once the party was coming to a close, I left and figured I would have more opportunities later.

I didn't take advantage of running around in expensive clothes, driving a Porsche 911 and staying in penthouse rooms by hitting the Miami nightclubs. Too many risks. I wasn't the perfect undercover agent. I did push the envelope on occasion, but I wasn't going to risk getting into trouble. The case agents were relying on me. Besides, I could lose future undercover roles. If the role required hitting the nightclubs, then I was all in.

One undercover role I accepted, which I can't talk about in detail, required me to enroll in a well-known college and take a graduate class to get close to a professor. I would join a fraternity and live on campus. While the case agent was establishing my background, I asked him, "How can I pass the exams?" I can barely spell cat, even if you spot me the C and the T. He told me he hadn't figured that out yet. I was still interested, but he needed to come up with a solid answer. This undercover role fell through. Maybe for the better.

In the meantime, during my Miami undercover role, the two case agents asked me to find out the owner and or manager of a particular business. They said the source would also be with me. This was early in the afternoon, and we all piled into one car and drove to a not so nice part of town. As we drove, I asked, "What exactly is the business?" They stopped in a parking and pointed across the street. I said, "You're kidding me, the strip club?" They explained that there was illegal activity occurring at this strip club, but they didn't provide any details, nor did I ask. The cash from the strip club was being laundered through the subject's financial institution. The case agents handed us cash. As the source and I were about to step out of the car, one of the agents said in a nonchalant manner, "By the way, the dancers in the club are all nude."

We walked in and sure enough, all nude. What was worse, there was only one other customer in the club so of course we attracted a small crowd of dancers. We both ordered drinks and watched the entertainment and surprisingly the dancers' appearances were better than what I expected. I don't recall how it happened, but about 30 to 45 minutes later, we walked out with the information. When we got into the car one of the case agents said, "We expected you guys to be there for a few hours." I simply said, "No," then gave him the information.

I rented a nice sized yacht so I could entertain my subjects and others while we cruised up and down the Florida* coast. We had champagne on ice and food at the ready, but at the last second the subjects called and canceled the cruise. Something unexpected happened at their office that they had to deal with. They apologized, but it was too late to cancel the cruise without forfeiting the entire amount, so the rest of us enjoyed the cruise, champagne and the fact that I didn't need to have my game face on. Another windshield day.

During this undercover role, while attending an invitation-only party, I was introduced to a 2000 Presidential primary candidate. To be clear, in no way was this individual involved in this case. I might have a picture shaking this person's hand.

This undercover role opened my eyes to the way rich people are treated. After staying on several occasions at the Luxury Hotel and always in one of the penthouse rooms, I called the hotel to set up another reservation for an upcoming trip. I told reservations that I needed to book a penthouse room for these dates. The lady that handled my call said the penthouse rooms were booked. She asked if I was interested in one of the regular rooms and I told her I was surprised because I never had this problem before. She asked if I had stayed in the penthouse rooms prior and asked for my name. When I provided my name (undercover name) she said hold for a moment. After less than a minute she came back and said I have you booked in one of the penthouse rooms. Could they have had a cancellation during that one minute I was on hold? Hmm.

On another occasion, I walked into the lobby to check in. The lobby and the front desk were small, but very nicely furnished as was the rest of the hotel. As I approached the front desk, a young woman behind the desk asked for my name on the reservation. As she did, I noticed the manager, who was standing a few feet behind her, tap her arm and pull her back a few feet from the counter. I overheard him say, "Don't you know who this guest is? He is so and so and is a regular guest in our penthouse rooms." The young woman stepped back to the counter and apologized and I immediately said it wasn't a big deal and not to worry about it. I felt bad for her. If the manager felt the need to say something, he should have done that in a more private setting.

I can't go into details about my meetings with the subjects, but I had a few good ones that had potential. Then, one day when I was in Dallas, I received a call from one of the case agents who said that they were shutting down the undercover operation immediately. I didn't receive details from him because the information was still fluid, but he indicated that the operation might have been accidentally compromised by the source. For safety and other reasons, the operation would be closed and the other undercover agent, whose only role was to have signature authority on the account, would withdraw the funds and close the account. I saw the case moving in the right direction, but these things can and do happen. I don't know what actually happened with the case. This happens sometimes. You just move on.

30

—◦•◦—

PHASE II – APPLICANT INTERVIEWS

One of my collateral duties, which I volunteered for, was called Phase II and I did this for 27 years. When I left the program, which was very close to my retirement, I was probably the most senior agent in the program. Phase II is the agent application interview and written test process, where Phase II agents, like me, sit on a three-agent panel and interview agent applicants. We also grade an applicant's handwritten test, which is based on a reading exercise. Once you're selected for this FBI program, you're trained in the applicant interview process, including the scoring of the interview. You're also trained on grading the applicant's handwritten exercise. I felt this collateral duty was equally as important as SWAT and undercover work. There were over 400 Phase II agents located throughout the FBI.

Around two years before my retirement, one of the support employees in the applicants unit at FBI Headquarters that I knew well, told me that the FBI was in the initial stages of making changes to the interview process. She asked if I was interested in spending at least three weeks at FBI Headquarters assisting in establishing the new interview process. I was honored to be asked and told her I needed to think about it due to time constraints. I knew in the back of my mind that I had too much case work to finish before retirement, so I turned it down.

In order for an agent applicant to reach the Phase II process they must go through a series of steps. First, the applicant must meet the FBI's basic requirements. There is a written test that probably hasn't changed much, including the approximate 50 percent pass rate. Sound simple? Throughout the entire process, the applicant is competing against other applicants located all over the country. What can the applicant bring to the FBI and does that meet the FBI's needs today?

The FBI office that you apply through will push their best applicants to FBI Headquarters in an attempt to get their applicant a Phase II interview. As I mentioned early in the book, when I was selected, and even today, only the top 4 percent of applicants were hired. The average hiring age for an agent is around 29 or 30. The more experience you have in a professional field, the greater chance of competing with other applicants. This is why I would strongly suggest that one shouldn't apply at an age of say 24 or 25. At 24 it's difficult to compete against the more experienced candidates. If you fail once, you only get a second shot at it, and that's only if the local office pushes your name through again.

During the 27 years I was a Phase II interviewer, more and more applicants had master's degrees. There was also a slight increase in PhDs. Just because you have a PhD doesn't mean you are ahead of the other applicants, though. Honestly, they just don't interview well for the agent position. I only recall passing two applicants who had PhDs. One hit it out of the park in the interview. I believe he received a perfect score. With his background and current job, which was impressive, I couldn't believe he wanted to be an FBI agent. During the Phase II interviews we could only ask each applicant the same very specific questions, so I didn't know what his thought process was. About six months after he graduated from the FBI Academy, I looked him up and learned that he had been assigned to a not so desirable FBI division. I called him and he said he remembered me from the interview. I told him that I was curious about why he wanted to be an FBI agent. He said that in the back of his mind he always had the desire to become an FBI agent. He impressed me again with that answer. He said that he was pleased with his decision and had no issues with his current assignment. All of this made me feel relieved and happy that I made that call.

Here are a few tips for interested agent candidates. I stress to the candidate in the beginning of the Phase II interview that we know nothing about them, which is true. We don't know where they went to school, their work experience, and so on. The interview is designed that way. All we have is a name when they walk into the interview room. There is very little personal chit chat, another design of the interview. There will be very little warming up for the interview with questions like, "Did you watch the Cowboys win the football game last night?" Or "What type of music do you like?" There are 13 questions, give or take one. Your only goal is to hit it out of the park with each answer. If you have positive life experiences and you know how to explain these experiences in a good amount of detail based on the questions, you should come out on top.

I can't mention any of the specific questions, but they generally can be answered using events that have occurred in your life. Here's a tip, which the FBI recruiter will likely tell you, your answers should have three parts: the situation, your actions and the outcome. Be prepared well before the interview. Think about all of your life events, which can include school, work, family, and so on. Then pick your best situations, actions and outcomes.

Numerous applicants I failed would give a detailed description of a situation, but very little about their own actions in that situation. This is a killer. Did you receive an award or save a person's life? Tell about those situations, not the ones where things went bad.

Good luck.

SHORT STORIES

31

---•·•---

ENVIRONMENTAL CRIMES CASES

The FBI has jurisdiction to investigate well over 300 federal violations and environmental crimes is one, which was popular in the 1990s. While I worked in the Memphis Division, I was either assigned or I developed numerous environmental crimes cases. I had a great working relationship with the Environmental Protection Agency (EPA) and various Tennessee state environmental government agencies. I formed a loose task force where we all shared resources and information that helped target and convict violators of EPA federal laws including violations such as the Clean Water Act. Back in the 1990s, environmental cases weren't a priority for the FBI, but we were able to pursue these cases if we had good cause. Today, very few of these cases are pursued by the FBI (the EPA is the lead in these cases). Of course, FBI case priorities changed across the board after 9/11. Even white-collar crimes cases were no longer the FBI's top priority.

I worked on several successful environment crimes cases with EPA agents. Even though, generally speaking, there aren't any direct victims of environmental crimes—you won't hear our oceans, rivers, waterways and soils complain—all of us are indirect victims.

In 1994, I opened an environmental crimes case in violation of Title 42 USC §6901 - Resource Conservation and Recovery Act (RCRA) on Jackson Johns*, the owner of a 55-gallon drum cleaning business, L & K Drum Cleaning* (LKDC), located in a poor black neighborhood in Memphis. I investigated this case with an EPA agent. LKDC was in business to clean and resell 55-gallon drums. The company was on 2.5

acres of land and at any given time, the site contained several thousand contaminated 55-gallon drums. The drums came in from almost empty to almost full of toxic and hazardous materials. The drums were cleaned on site with high pressure washers and steam that caused the waste to go directly into the grounds at LKDC. Johns held no permits for hazardous waste storage nor transportation. People residing in the neighborhood complained about the smell and the constant yellow and orange mist that hung in the air and coated their porches. They couldn't enjoy an evening sitting on their front porches.

This case attracted the attention of the DOJ and the United States Attorney for the Western District of Tennessee. A DOJ attorney and the United States Attorney would prosecute this case. In my 31 years I have only had two United States Attorneys who were the prosecutors in my cases, instead of the usual AUSA.

Since this was back in the 1990s, I was out knocking on the doors of these residences, dressed in my suit. I stood out in this almost all black neighborhood and I was only able to get a small number of people to open the door and speak to me. One of the homes was across the street and the closest residence to LKDC. I knocked on the door the first time and the lady inside wouldn't open the door even after I identified myself and held up my credentials to the peephole. I came back the next day and again knocked and this time she cracked the door open, and I briefly spoke to her about why I was there. I tried my charm, but apparently it wasn't enough, because she didn't invite me in or come out to visit. The next day I was knocking on other residences' doors and I thought I would try her door again. It would help the case to get witnesses who would testify if needed in trial about how LKDC directly hindered their lives. Jury appeal. On this occasion, I knocked on the door and she again cracked the door and I told her that I could see the yellow and orange residue on her porch. I explained that I was here to help rid the neighborhood of this company, but I needed her help. She let me in her home – third time's a charm – and even though she was reserved she told me how miserable her life was living across the street from LKDC.

One day I had our Memphis FBI pilot fly me over the LKDC site to take photographs to be used as evidence. I remember that day because it was a hot summer day and I was flying in a small two-seater. All of a sudden I sat straight up and was sweating profusely and no longer looking down. The FBI agent pilot recognized this and asked me what was wrong. I told him I wasn't feeling well, but I wanted him to make another pass over the site so that I could get a few more photographs. He said, "No, we're flying back to the landing strip because I don't want you to throw up in my plane." I didn't blame him. When we landed, I went directly to his office and lay down on his couch and it took me a few hours to recover from the air sickness. I was happy that he made that quick and correct decision. But I did get my photographs. (See the picture section of the book.)

After gathering overwhelming evidence, Johns was convicted and sentenced to serve 41 months in a federal prison, which at the time, according to the DOJ, was equal to the largest sentence imposed in an RCRA case. The 2.5-acre LKDC site became a $1.5 million Superfund EPA cleanup site. During the clean-up, over 10,000 tons of soil was removed, which included oils and hydrocarbons down to five feet.

Several months later I was walking to lunch, dressed in my suit, in downtown Memphis when I heard someone call out my name. The streets were crowded, but as I turned, I saw the lady who, after three tries, had let me in her residence to interview her. She came walking up to me with a smile and gave me a quick hug and thanked me for the job I did. She said that after the Superfund cleanup, she was able to enjoy sitting on her porch. I truly felt good for her and myself. I was definitely the windshield that day.

I had other successful environmental cases. In 1991, I investigated Kodo Inks*, an ink company that was located on a tributary of the Mississippi River in Memphis. During the production of inks, the subjects discharged solvents and ink wash into the tributary in violation of Title 33 USC §1251 the Clean Water Act (CWA) and illegally stored hazardous waste without a permit in violation of the RCRA. There were four subjects in this case and one of them tried to protect his boss by lying to me in the interview, which was a violation of Title 18 USC §1001, false statements to an FBI agent. This was my first conviction of a person making a false statement to me in an investigation. I guess he took one for the team. The sad ending for him was that he received a stiffer sentence than his boss. All pled guilty (no trial). In the sentencing phase, I had the AUSA force Kodo Inks to place a full-page ad in the *Memphis Commercial Appeal* newspaper apologizing to the citizens of Memphis for polluting the environment and explaining that they would pay a $200,000 fine. I had heard about doing something like this during an environmental crimes training class.

While I worked on these environment cases I had limited gear to wear if I was to walk on a hazardous material site. Later, while on the SWAT team, I trained at Quantico and was certified in a Weapons of Mass Destruction (WMD) class and received much better hazardous material equipment, including a level 4 hazmat suit and related clothing.

32

<hr />

ANTITRUST CASES

While in the FBI Dallas Division, I worked from 1999 to 2006 as the detail FBI agent assigned to the Dallas Antitrust office in downtown Dallas. My office was on the 49th floor of a high-rise with a great view of Dallas. I had assigned parking in the basement garage, an FBI requirement for our FBI vehicles. At the time, there were about six of these offices in the United States. The antitrust detail assignments were established between FBI Headquarters and the Antitrust Division in Washington DC. The detail agent exclusively investigated antitrust criminal cases. Even though I worked on these cases exclusively, I still had three collateral duties that pulled me out of the antitrust office from time to time. Plus like any other agent, I had to respond to large events where the FBI had an interest or the lead investigation. Such as 9/11.

Even though there were about six offices in the United States, I only recall about three or four agents assigned to investigate these matters. This was an assignment I requested. The prior Dallas detail agent was getting burned out on the amount of travel required, since he had a family. The agent was required to travel to any and all interviews, versus sending out leads to other FBI divisions for coverage, which was the normal FBI procedure unless it was a subject interview. The Antitrust Division paid all travel expenses and I always traveled with at least one DOJ antitrust attorney. The Dallas antitrust office had a region that covered Texas and the four surrounding states. But my travel was all over the United States and one trip outside the United States to Madrid, Spain to interview a hostile witness. I made over 130 trips while I was the detail agent. This amount of travel plus my three collateral duties was an enormous, time-consuming workload. I had a tremendous working relationship with these dedicated DOJ attorneys.

What are antitrust criminal cases? These fall under what is known as the Sherman Antitrust Act, which is a federal statute that prohibits businesses from colluding to fix prices, divide markets/territories and rig bids. A simple example of an antitrust violation would be as follows: XYZ brand of a gallon of milk is sold at five different grocery store chains. These grocery store chains communicate and collude to keep the price of this gallon of milk at, say $4.00. They then agree to raise the price of this gallon of milk .20 cents every six months. Here's another example: These same grocery store chains divide the territory in Dallas, meaning they agree not to build their grocery store brand in another grocery store's designated territory. That way, one store chain can raise their prices without fear of price competition on their products. If these laws are overlooked and not enforced, think about how much the consumer would pay for their everyday products.

When I had information to open an antitrust investigation outside the FBI Dallas Division AO, I had to call the appropriate FBI office to offer that office the case. Each time these offices said that I could open and investigate the case. These other FBI divisions knew little to nothing about antitrust violations. But each time I made a trip to their AO, I would email the SSA of the white-collar crime squad that technically handled antitrust cases to advise of my travel into their AO. This was basic FBI policy and courtesy, even though my jurisdiction was the entire United States and its territories.

On one occasion I was preparing to interview, with the assistance of three DOJ antitrust attorneys, a Japanese executive of a large corporation. He and his staff had flown in from Japan for this meeting at the Dallas antitrust office. He was cooperating in a large antitrust case of mine. The subject companies were located in Japan but were violating our antitrust laws. This meeting was held in the plush DOJ antitrust conference room with other Japanese executives and a Japanese translator. Including myself and the three DOJ attorneys, there were at least 10 individuals in the meeting. We were all dressed in suits. As the meeting began, I presented my credentials to the Japanese executive as required. He was sitting directly across from me next to his translator. The atmosphere was professional, but standoffish. After I sat back down the Japanese executive said something to the translator in Japanese and the translator asked me if I could show the executive my credentials again. The room was quiet as all eyes were on me. I opened my credentials and laid them on the table in front of the executive. He picked up my credentials, stood up and flashed them like you see in the movies and said with a tough voice in broken English, "FBI, FBI! Put your hands up!" After the shock wore off, we all laughed and the ice was broken. I guess, even in Japan, they watch too many FBI shows and movies.

In most of the antitrust cases the subjects are the actual companies versus individuals. I successfully investigated cases that involved price fixing the manufacture of Vitamins, Polyester Staple and many other goods. Many of these companies were well known companies located in Europe and Asia that sold products in the United States. All of the companies pled guilty and were levied large fines. During the years I investigated antitrust violations my cases netted over $200 million in fines.

33

<hr/>

JORDAN, MONTANA STANDOFF

In May 1996, while I was in the Memphis FBI office, our SWAT team was called up to travel to Jordan, Montana to respond to the "Montana Freemen" standoff with the United States government. Several groups of FBI SWAT teams were rotating in and out of Jordan during an 81-day standoff. The Freemen group basically wanted to self-govern and didn't believe in the laws of the United States. They committed several bank fraud violations and several had already been arrested, but the rest of the group held out in a remote area outside of Jordan. They had various posts set up to monitor any approach we might use in an attempt to arrest the group. The land was mostly flat with little to no foliage and their residence and various posts were on inclines that enabled them to have an advantage, especially since they had high power scoped rifles compared to the handguns we were allowed to carry.

The FBI's approach was directed by the DOJ, through United States Attorney General Janet Reno. Many of Reno's decisions were based on the action and the outcome of the FBI standoff with the Branch Davidians in Waco, Texas, which ended in a mass murder suicide committed by the leader David Koresh, similar to Jonestown. Based on this, Reno didn't want the FBI to attempt to arrest the Freemen. Instead, we were placed as far away as a mile from the Freemen's residence. We were limited to only our handguns and other light gear. Several of the guys on the various SWAT teams, including myself, were concerned with the unnecessary danger that Reno subjected us to. We weren't allowed to have an Air Ambulance nearby to respond to any serious injury. The closest Air Ambulance was too far away to properly respond to any real medical emergency. There was a lot of ill talk about Reno and the ridiculous decisions she was making.

Our SWAT team packed up and drove our vehicles from Memphis to the small town of Jordan. Jordan, with a population of about 400, is located in the Eastern part of the state and the closest decent-sized town is about 85 miles away. The FBI and the news media flooded Jordan. If I recall, there was one streetlight, one gas station, two bars and two motels. This was my first trip to Montana, and I always pictured Montana as lush and covered with Mountains. Not this part of the state; it was very flat.

We stayed in a shack and slept on cots. Each morning we drove to the command post, the Garfield County Fairgrounds, which was established in a large barn where local volunteers cooked us breakfast and coffee. The volunteers were friendly, supportive and accommodating. The SWAT teams were positioned all around the Freemen's residence, but a distance away. We watched the residence 24 hours a day, 7 days a week. We worked different shifts. The drive from the command post to our SWAT team posts was over 30 minutes long through winding dirt and gravel roads. A few weeks prior to our arrival in Jordan, an FBI SWAT team member from another office lost control of his vehicle on one of these roads and flipped it. He was found dead near his vehicle. A sad and tragic accident. Over the years we have lost far too many SWAT team agents to training accidents and friendly fire.

On numerous occasions, when we were on our established roadblock, locals slowly approached us in their vehicles and provided us with cooked meals. This community was gracious and welcoming. Without a doubt the local economy soared during those 81 days. There was always a line of FBI and news media vehicles at the gas station and each night the two bars were full, as if we were in a large city. I know the community enjoyed our company and the excitement. The FBI SWAT team members were popular, but I'm sure after a while the community wanted to get back to their quiet lives. Nothing of substance happened while we were in Jordan and when our assignment ended, we headed back to Memphis. Including our drive, I was in Jordan for 21 days. A few weeks later the Freemen group surrendered; some received very stiff sentences.

1996 was a very busy year for me, which included the Atlanta

Summer Olympics, travel to Barbados to conduct search warrants, travel for SWAT to Jordan, Montana, one week in Louisiana and one week in Alabama for SWAT training, one week in New York City and one week in Los Angeles for Phase II interviews.

34

<hr/>

GRACELAND

During the 10 years I was assigned to the Memphis Division, I had never visited Graceland, until an odd phone call came into the Memphis FBI office one day in the 1990s. The call was from one of Elvis Presley's relatives working security at Graceland. He told us that a fugitive portrayed on a recent "America's Most Wanted" episode was currently walking on a Graceland VIP tour. I was quickly assigned to this lead. I contacted security at Graceland to meet this relative and join the VIP tour. I grabbed another agent and we gathered the photographs and identifiers of the fugitive in question and placed the information in a folder. Dressed in our suits, we removed our ties and drove the 15 minutes from the downtown office to Graceland to meet with the relative. When we arrived, this relative quickly escorted us through the Graceland home and we caught up with the VIP tour group, which included approximately 25 tourists. He discreetly pointed out the individual in question and the other agent and I immediately thought this was *not* in fact the fugitive.

We caught up to this individual and followed him and his female companion for several minutes and had several good looks at his face and other physical features. The other agent and I pulled off to the side for a minute and reviewed the photographs and agreed that the individual in question didn't match the actual fugitive. But we still needed to actually identify the person in question, so we continued with the tour and waited for our chance to approach him. The chance came while the individual and his female companion were observing Elvis Presley's grave. What a peculiar place to pull out our credentials and question someone. After we identified ourselves, they were both very startled. *Elvis' grave, FBI agents in suits, what the heck was this?* I explained that the FBI office received an "anonymous" tip regarding an "America's Most Wanted" fugitive and we requested his identification. He provided his driver's license and other identifiers. We looked closely at his license and his actual appearance and confirmed that he wasn't the fugitive in question.

I'm sure their Graceland tour was a little more exciting than what they expected. And now they had a better Graceland tour story to share with family and friends. We thanked the relative and returned to the FBI office. I guess you could say I had a free VIP tour of the Graceland home and grounds. After looking through the home, it was a flashback to my 1970s.

35

—◦·◦—

FUGITIVE SHOT AND ARRESTED

Late on a Friday night, in the fall of 1996, while I was a member of the Memphis FBI SWAT team, I received an immediate call out from the SWAT team leader. The Memphis FBI received information that a UFAP out of North Carolina*, wanted for the rape and murder of two women, was residing in a small shed at a steel and sheet metal company located off a rural road northeast of Memphis. I joined with other Memphis FBI SWAT team members to rally at a designated point established by the team leader who began briefing the SWAT team members and the arrest plan. It began to rain lightly. It was now getting close to 1:00 AM.

The local Sheriff's department was in place to block any east and west traffic on the rural road, which ran in front of the steel and sheet metal company. The SWAT team leader, another SWAT team member and I set up on the east side of the shed, approximately 30 yards away. Our priority was to watch an RV trailer located approximately 15 to 20 yards behind the shed. Closely behind us were stacks of scrap metal. The shed was being covered on the west side by other SWAT team members. The rain began falling harder. When the arrest execute order was given via radio, other SWAT team members began to approach the front of the shed, utilizing a PA from one of our vehicles. I heard an agent call out the fugitive's name on the PA system and say that the FBI had the shed surrounded and to come out with his hands up. As the agent's voice echoed the fugitive's name, the commands over the PA grew louder and more rapid, "Put your hands up, put your hands up!" At this point I expected to hear gunfire, which I did. As the gunfire began, I heard the rounds hitting the scrap metal behind us. We immediately went prone to avoid being hit by these rounds. Simultaneously, a light in the RV trailer came on and the trailer door opened, which faced the shed. We stood back up, ignoring the rounds hitting behind us, to intercept whoever was coming out that trailer door. We ran toward the individual and ordered him to the ground. He complied and we cuffed and searched him for safety reasons, then later released him. We heard on the radio that the fugitive was shot and was down and an agent had also been hit, but the fugitive was in custody. The "all clear" was given, so we immediately gathered in front of the shed. An ambulance was called to the scene. The agent had been hit in the face by a ricochet, but only needed treatment at the scene. The fugitive was hit several times, including a 10 mm round in the chest.

I was told by the SWAT team leader to advise the FBI office. I radioed the office and advised that we had been involved in a shooting. The office made contact with the Memphis SAC and I was told to call the SAC at home, which I did via telephone. With the lack of agents on the scene I was told to ride in the ambulance with the fugitive, who was now in my custody. A Tennessee Bureau of Investigation (TBI) agent accompanied me to the hospital, which was approximately 30 minutes away. I rode in the front seat, while the TBI agent rode in the back with the subject. I remember this ambulance ride because the rain was now pouring down. The ambulance driver buried his foot on the gas pedal as we were moving up and down rolling hills. I had a feeling he was trying to impress me with his driving speed. I looked over at the speedometer and saw that it was over 100 mph. With the pouring rain and the road conditions I aggressively told the ambulance driver to back off the speed, which he did after a short argument. We arrived at the hospital and they rushed the fugitive into surgery while we remained in the hospital.

The doctor eventually came out of surgery and asked me to join him in an x-ray room. The doctor indicated that he knew the patient was a fugitive and was wanted for murders and rapes. He told me that the fugitive would survive his wounds even though he arrived in critical condition. The doctor also told me that he counted at least 12 wounds. The doctor showed me the x-rays and pointed to a 10 mm round that was lodged very close to the fugitive's heart. In so many words, he indicated that we had just missed.

I remained at the hospital until almost mid-morning and was given a ride back to my car at our rally point. I was dead tired, but I stopped at the scene of the shooting to see if any of the agents needed assistance. I finally returned home late that Saturday morning. I returned to the office that Monday and was told that due to FBI policy, I would be put on administrative leave for three days, because of being involved on the scene of a shooting. The FBI "shoot team" would be flying in from Quantico, which is the norm for conducting an investigation. I could understand being interviewed by the shoot team but couldn't believe a psychiatrist had to interview me about my thoughts and feelings. Really? I thought *it was a waste of time*. I had no problem with what happened on scene.

This was not the only time I was involved in a shooting; there were two more. Once, while on the Memphis SWAT team, we were chasing a wanted bank robber when the bank robber turned to engage the pursuing agents. He was shot by an agent with a shotgun. He survived his wounds, probably lucky for him that the agent fired a buckshot round instead of a slug round. The other time was while I was on the Dallas FBI SWAT team. In both of these agent-involved shootings, I was not placed on administrative leave, nor was I interviewed by a psychiatrist. I was, however, interviewed by our "shoot team."

36

---◦•◦---

UNABOM, AKA UNABOMBER

In May of 1995, I volunteered for a one-month assignment in San Francisco to assist in the Unabomber investigation. The Unabomber was a domestic terrorist who mailed or delivered 16 different bombs between 1978 to 1995, only two of which were defused. Three people were killed and 23 wounded in these attacks. The Unabomber was against the advancements in technology and industry that he felt was harming the environment.

The San Francisco FBI office was leading the investigation. In 1995, when I arrived in San Francisco, the FBI didn't have the Unabomber's name and only had very little identifying information. The FBI felt that the Unabomber was residing in Northern California, specifically around the San Francisco area. The FBI had a crude drawing of what the Unabomber might look like, the type of typewriter he was using, some personality traits based on profiling, and little else. Numerous agents had traveled from various FBI Divisions to work this temporary assignment in San Francisco. I was partnered with an agent from another FBI office to cover leads by locating and interviewing individuals whose names came from the tip line the FBI had established for this case. We were briefed on what to look for based on the information and the approach the FBI was taking to identify the Unabomber. We were given the information from the tip, the name of the person in question and an address and told to go and cover these leads. We were to locate and interview these people to determine if they could be an actual suspect or remove them from the list.

Each morning my partner and I arrived at the San Francisco office and picked up our leads to be covered for the day. At the time, the agent assigning the leads was not from the San Francisco area, and in 1995, we didn't have GPS or Google maps. We looked at the address, found it on a paper map and made a plan that would route us in the most logical manner. We were generally given five to ten leads a day. These locations were literally scattered all over the San Francisco Bay area. It would have made more sense if the agent assigning these leads was from the San Francisco office. No matter, we enjoyed driving all over the bay area seeing the various sites.

The only lead we thought matched the Unabomber profile based on information given to us became even more encouraging after we entered this person's home and spoke with him. We observed items within his residence that met priority items to look for based on his profile. Also, when we interviewed him, he was so nervous, he couldn't hold his cereal spoon, though that was somewhat expected based on the questions we were asking. Most of these leads and tips were far-fetched, but we still had to cover them to eliminate the person in question. After my month concluded, I packed up and returned to Memphis.

One year later, FBI agents arrested Ted Kaczynski at his cabin in a remote part of Montana. Kaczynski received a sentence of eight life sentences.

37

---·◦·---

HOLY LAND FOUNDATION
TERRORISM CASE

From 2006 to 2010, I was assigned to a Counter Terrorism (CT) squad as one of the case agents for to the Holy Land Foundation investigation. This was a new assignment for me, since I had investigated white-collar crime cases for the past 17 years. The squad was located in a Sensitive Compartmented Information Facility (SCIF) in the Dallas Headquarters office. It wasn't an assignment I wanted with my skillset and background, but it turned out to be worthwhile and beneficial for my career. I was given a Top Secret Sensitive Compartmented Information clearance, which I held through my retirement. I honestly didn't like working in the SCIF room. I just called it a lockdown. There were strict rules like no cell phones and no laptops, and a constant flow of Top-Secret documents across my desk. This just wasn't my cup of tea.

Two years later, after another background investigation, I received a "Q" clearance, so that I, along with other members of the Dallas FBI SWAT team, could tour the Pantex Plant located outside of Amarillo, Texas, for possible operational purposes. This plant is the nation's primary facility for the final assembly, dismantlement and maintenance of nuclear weapons. It was an eye-opening tour. We briefly trained with the Department of Energy teams while we were in Amarillo. Their deadly force policy is understandably different from ours. Ours is along the lines of surgical shooting, whereas they're protecting a much bigger prize. Understandably, they have no problem using deadly force if needed, even when there are innocent parties in the way, to protect our nuclear weapons.

When I was assigned to the CT squad and the Holy Land Foundation case I was totally behind the curve. The other four FBI case agents had been working on this case for years. I, however, was the most experienced of the five case agents in financial investigations. This was a terrorism financing investigation. I reviewed a lot of financial records and later worked with the prosecution team in preparation for trial. I spent over three years on this team and sometimes we worked seven days a week at the United States Attorney's office in Dallas. I couldn't have worked with a more dedicated group. I was astonished by the knowledge that two of the agents had regarding terrorist groups around the world and the Holy Land Foundation case.

The five subjects of Holy Land Foundation were eventually charged and convicted of 10 counts of material support to the terrorist organization, Hamas, each receiving a sentence of 15 to 65 years, including a $12.4 million judgment. This case made world news. I won't go into the details of the case, for obvious reasons, but a simple Google search of Holy Land Foundation can give you the basics.

After the convictions, the United States Attorney/prosecutor and the two DOJ attorneys recommended the entire team for the United States Attorney General's Distinguished Service Award, which is the most prestigious award an FBI agent can receive. The recommendations are sent to the DOJ Washington DC office and from there the selection process begins. Our team didn't know if the recommendations would be approved. After waiting a few months, we learned that we were all selected to receive the award for our work in this case. We were flown to Washington DC to be presented with our awards by the United States Attorney General in a ceremony held in DAR Constitution Hall. There were other groups receiving the AG award as well. The event, food, and the Marine Band playing at the ceremony were all quite spectacular. We were allowed to bring one guest and I brought my mother, who was overwhelmed by the whole process. My dad had passed away seven years prior, but I know my mother felt his presence in living his dream through me.

A short time later, I was offered, and I accepted my transfer to the Frisco RA, where I spent my last 10 years in luxury.

38

COLLATERAL DUTIES

I had three collateral duties during my career: I was a member of the Memphis and Dallas FBI SWAT Teams from late 1990 to 2009; took on various undercover roles between 1992 and 2017; and participated in Phase II from 1995 to 2018. I wasn't paid extra for any of these collateral duties. All three duties required training and certification. It was unusual for an agent to actively work three collateral duties simultaneously along with their full-time case work. Many agents don't volunteer for one collateral duty, let alone three. At one point in the Dallas office, one of our ASACs sent out an email that stated agents could only have up to two collateral duties because of the burden it places on their case work. Following this email, I met with that ASAC and he told me that I was keeping up with all of my work and doing a good job, so he allowed me to continue with my three collateral duties.

Agents aren't paid extra for collateral duties, but depending on the duty, it takes up a lot of your time. While on the SWAT team for 18 years our training increased over time. We trained from one to three times a month depending on what was scheduled. The training might require one day or a week in another location. Then there were missions that would take a minimum of two days. My undercover roles were inconsistent. One year I might spend days, weeks or few months in the roles. Phase II was my most consistent collateral duty. Phase II agents could basically pick and choose when (based on the interview schedules) and where they would conduct the Phase II interviews, which were generally located in eight or nine FBI Divisions throughout the country.

For Phase II, in the early years, I traveled five times per year (five weeks). And later, on average, I traveled three times per year (three weeks). So you can see how my collateral duties were an enormous expenditure of time. There are other collateral duties available to FBI agents, including Firearms Instructor and Evidence Response Team. The agents who didn't have collateral duties were known in the offices and discussed amongst the agents that carried the extra load. Some SSAs recognized this and would pursue these agents to volunteer to work search warrants, arrests, "sitting on a wire" (wiretaps) and other extra duties.

39

WEAPON AND CREDENTIAL MISHAPS

When I entered the FBI in 1988, retiring FBI agents had to turn in their badges and credentials. These badges remained in a safe at FBI Headquarters until the badges were reissued to new agents. I don't know when this changed, but it was after 1988. Today, retiring FBI agents must return their badge and credentials to FBI Headquarters, but Headquarters will frame their badge and credentials in a nice shadow box case so that you can display it. When I received my badge at my graduation in 1988, I noticed that it was badly tarnished compared to other agent's badges. Around five years later, I contacted the FBI Headquarters unit that issues badges and spoke to a very understanding and nice lady in the unit. She had me fill out paperwork to return my badge and she would reissue me a different one. While I was on the telephone with her, she asked if I wanted a newer or an older badge. I told her the older the better. She told me that she had a badge that was produced in January 1941, and first issued in 1944 (during World War II). The last agent who carried the badge returned it in 1992. She provided the names of the agents who carried this badge from 1944 to 1992. I felt honored to receive badge number 1549, which had a lengthy history associated with it. Especially since I have studied World War II history since my early teens. I have read over 150 World War II books and consider myself well-versed in World War II history. My badge and credentials are now proudly displayed at my home.

When I went through the FBI academy in 1988, we were taught how important and personal weapons and credentials are to each agent. They were correct. I protected both with a passion. Back then, if you lost either your weapon or your credentials you received an automatic one month off (without pay). It was a blemish in your file. I believe now you only receive a "letter of censor." On one occasion, I lost my credentials at the federal building in downtown Memphis for a few hours. I had been downstairs visiting others in the break room. I had taken my jacket off and placed it around my chair. My credentials were in the front inside pocket, which is where we were taught to keep them. I went upstairs and was working at my desk when I realized I didn't have my jacket. I ran downstairs and learned that the break room was locked and closed for the night. I found security told him that I needed to get in the break room now and not tomorrow and after he opened the door there was my jacket and credentials. I dodged a bullet there.

This happened only one other time to me, and it was, by far, much worse. While I was in the Dallas FBI division, I had flown to Houston with a DOJ Attorney to conduct an interview and we would return to Dallas the next day. That next morning we checked out of our hotel rooms and boarded the airport shuttle, which was about a 30-minute drive. As we were pulling into the airport, I realized I didn't have my weapon. I said to the DOJ Attorney, "Oh shit, I have to get back to the hotel. Looks like I won't be on the flight with you."

He wished me luck and I jumped in a cab and asked the cab driver to get me to the hotel as quickly as possible. During the ride I called the hotel and identified myself and told them to quickly put someone from security on the phone. I spoke to the security officer of the hotel and after identifying myself, explained that I had just checked out of my hotel room, but left something of high importance in the room which was for my eyes only. I said, "Don't allow the hotel cleaning staff to enter the room." He understood, but said he wasn't sure if the cleaning staff had already entered my room. Bad thoughts were going through my mind in this long and agonizing cab ride. My credentials aren't deadly, but this weapon with no safety and a round in the chamber could be bad news.

I arrived at the hotel and ran to my room. I still had the plastic key card. I opened the door and joyfully noticed that my bed was unmade, and no cleaning staff had entered. But where was my gun and holster? As I looked and looked, panic resurfaced. I looked in the bathroom, even under the bed. I sat on the bed and was thinking where the heck could it be. I moved the bedspread cover back and there she was. I thought about kissing it. I put the holster and gun on. I called security and told him all was good and thanked him several times. I took a cab back to the airport with a round trip expense of $100. It was the best $100 I had ever spent. I missed my flight, but simply caught the next flight back to Dallas. Thankfully, we can change our flights at the drop of a hat without paying extra.

If I had not recovered my weapon, this would have prompted a problematic and embarrassing domino effect. My first call would have been hotel security, then my SSA. My SSA would have to call the Dallas ASAC and the SAC would have been notified. What would have been worse is that this was in another FBI Division - Houston. Their office would be contacted by Dallas management and agents would be sent to the hotel for a search and interviews of staff etc. I would have received time off and a bad reputation in both Dallas and Houston. Word would have spread.

I was almost the bug.

While I was Acting SSA on my squad for a miserable six-month period in Memphis (I totally disliked being an SSA), a new agent straight out of the FBI academy arrived and was assigned to my squad. He walked into my office, introduced himself and said, "I just graduated from the FBI academy. The office is expecting me and I'm reporting for duty, but I lost my credentials." I said, "What do you mean? How?" He said he and his wife had been at their apartment unpacking boxes, but they couldn't locate his credentials. I said, "I don't want to introduce you to the ASAC and say this is the new agent right out of the FBI academy, oh, and by the way, he lost his credentials."

I explained to the new agent that you don't want to start your career like that. I told him to go home and look for his credentials and that he had 24 hours. About five hours later he called and told me they still couldn't find his credentials. I said, "You still have time, don't give up yet." A few hours later he gave up and came back into the office. I walked him up to the ASAC's office and introduced him to the ASAC as our new agent and said, "He has lost his credentials." I turned around and walked away. I don't know what happened to him for losing his credentials. Years later, I learned that while he was in another FBI Division, he was part of a team that successfully convicted subjects of a large corporation that made national news. Glad to hear he bounced back.

40

---◦·◦---

SPECIALIZED SWAT TRAINING

I was a member of the Memphis and Dallas SWAT teams for a total of 18 years and received the following SWAT training: Basic and Advanced SWAT Training, Weapons of Mass Destruction, Basic and Advanced Combat Shooting, Basic and Advanced Tracking School, Defensive Shooting (Mid-South Institute of Self Defense Shooting), Active Shooter, Aircraft/Bus/Train Tactical Entry, Active Marine Vessel Tactical Entry, Deploying Tactics from Huey Helicopter, Land Navigation, Basic Medical, and other related training.

As I mentioned earlier, I didn't have a military or police background. On my first day of SWAT training, while assigned to the Memphis office, the team traveled to Nashville to conduct "room clears" in an abandoned hospital that had been provided to us. There were numerous rooms and many pieces of antiquated hospital equipment. We weren't allowed to fire our weapons inside the hospital.

When we first entered, two other members of the SWAT team and I were standing in the lobby when another member said, "Let's test a flashbang in the lobby." Not knowing at the time what a flashbang was, I stood there as the other agent pulled the pin and tossed the flashbang within 20 feet of where I was standing. Out of the corner of my eyes I could see the other members retreat, but it was too late for me. The explosion flashed with an enormous concussion, made louder by the fact that we were in an enclosed room. Everyone but me had a nice laugh. A mishap using a flashbang could cause the loss of body parts or even death.

This was my welcome to the SWAT team.

Later, while on the Dallas SWAT team, we were conducting room clears at Ft Hood, Texas military base utilizing a ballistic shield and flashbangs. I was crouched, holding the shield with another agent behind me. The agent behind me threw a flashbang that was supposed to go into another room, but instead it hit the doorframe and bounced back, landing a foot from me. The other agent retreated, but I had no time to retreat. Without panicking, I held the shield tight and angled it downward over the flashbang. Thankfully, the concussion from the blast merely numbed me for a few minutes. After spouting a few nasty words towards the other agent, we laughed about it later. All part of training.

While on the Memphis FBI SWAT team in the 1990s, I trained with other Memphis SWAT team members at the Mid-South Institute of Self Defense Shooting (MSISDS) located approximately 35 minutes south of Memphis. We were regulars there. At the time, two-time world pistol silver medalist John Shaw owned and operated the shooting facility. This amazing facility covered several acres and had many shoot houses, shooting alleys and moving targets. I really enjoyed the moving targets aspect of our training. In real life, targets are not going to stand still and let you put holes in them. I can say without doubt my shooting skills were at their highest level after training under Shaw and his staff. I witnessed another expert shooter on the staff throw rocks in the air, shoot at and hit those rocks.

Each time Shaw competed against eight to ten members of our SWAT team in a pistol speed competition with eight-inch round metal targets, he won. He was one shooter, and we were eight or ten with the same number of targets. Still, he won easily every time. I couldn't believe how quickly he brought those targets down. I would say it was embarrassing, but he was one of the top pistol shooters in the world. He and his staff would put pressure on us when we walked an alley with multiple targets by yelling at us and throwing small rocks at us to cause confusion and increase the pressure, so it was more like a real-world environment. I was amazed at how much better my shooting speed became and how quickly I was able to change magazines and "get back into the fight" without taking my eyes off other targets and threats. MSISDS only trains United States Military, Federal, State and Local law enforcement. They also trained the United States Special Operations Force (special ops).

During my career, my cases included the investigations of a variety of federal violations. Some of these cases are discussed in this book. Other cases I successfully investigated included the following violations: Telemarketing Fraud, Civil Rights, Fraud against the Federal Government, Bank Fraud, Public Corruption of Elected Officials, Mortgage Fraud, Healthcare Fraud, Money Laundering in a Criminal Organization, Wire Fraud, Corporate Fraud, Bankruptcy Fraud and an Office of Professional Responsible Investigation of another Federal Agent.

"A good agent does not go to trial."